EXPOSING
NORTHERN EXPOSURE

WELCOME
TO
CICELY, ALASKA
POP. ~~214~~ 215   ELEV 6,572

Scott Nance

Books for the entertainment buyer

PIONEER

Library of Congress Cataloging-in-Publication Data
Scott Nance—
    Exposing Northern Exposure

    1.   Exposing Northern Exposure (popular culture)
  I. Title

Published by Pioneer Books, Inc., 5715 N. Balsam Rd., Las Vegas, NV, 89130.

First Printing, 1992

Dedicated to the spirit of the wilderness

Many special thanks need to be given to Andy Bates for his great time and effort on the episode guide. Thanks also to An Oasis president Anthony Burokas. The Burson-Marsteller P.R. firm was very helpful in providing much of the information herein.

Sources cited include the Associated Press, *IN Fashion* magazine, *New York* magazine, *People* magazine, the *New York Times*, and the *Seattle Times*.

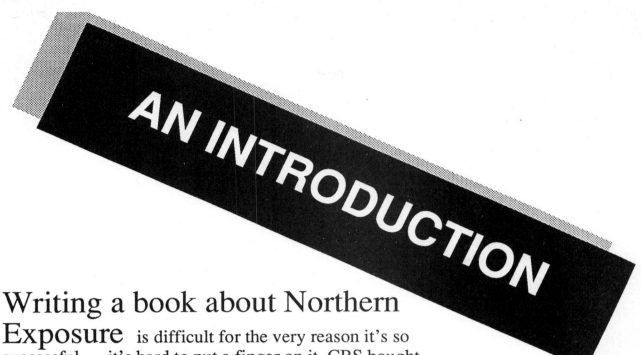

Writing a book about Northern Exposure

is difficult for the very reason it's so successful. . . it's hard to put a finger on it. CBS bought it from creators Josh Brand and John Falsey with just one descriptive phrase: "New York doctor in small-town Alaska." That doesn't begin to tell the tale of the quirky town of Cicely, Alaska.

The details seem simple enough: the state of Alaska pays for Dr. Joel Fleischman's medical school education in exchange for four years of service. As the series opens, the doctor is flying to Alaska expecting an easy assignment in the city of Anchorage. That changes when he is assigned to the remote rural community of Cicely. There he meets the oddball residents of the town.

There is ex-astronaut Maurice who dreams of the day when Cicely is part of the "Alaskan Riviera." Maggie the bush pilot whom Joel rankles immediately by mistaking her for a prostitute. Holling is the aging barkeep with an eighteen-year-old girlfriend named Shelly. Chris is the disc jockey who quotes Jung and Whitman on the air. Ed is a young Indian who dreams of being the next Fellini. Then there is silent but sage Marilyn who insists on working as his medical assistant.

Brand gets close to the soul, saying, "The town is a

non-judgemental place. There's never any intent to hurt or expose. A lot of the show is hung on that. That idyllic existence is contrasted with crotchety Joel Fleischman. "The function of Joel's character is he provides ballast," said Brand. "He adds a certain skepticism that you have to bring to things."

It still feels like there's something missing. I hope that by bringing together so many elements in this book, that we might get a little closer to Cicely, Alaska.

THE SHOW

SHOW NOTES

When first telecast on CBS in July, 1990, *Northern Exposure* was a critically acclaimed but virtually unknown summer series with a moose as a mascot. Since then, the series now known for its quirky characters and unique plot twists has continued to grow in popularity, garnering rave reviews, successful ratings, and several Emmy nominations. Some of the shows awards includes Outstanding Drama Series and Outstanding Writing in a Drama Series.

After a six-month hiatus the series returned in March, 1991 to its Monday night timeslot. *Northern Exposure* has continually won its time period and consistently remains in the top ten rated shows each week.

Northern Exposure is a one-hour drama/comedy set in the fictional town of Cicely, Alaska, where life borders on the eccentric and basic comforts are scarce. The quirky series focuses on the trials and tribulations of Dr. Joel Fleishman (Rob Morrow), an inveterate New Yorker who has been reluctantly transplanted to the remote Alaskan town. He made a deal with the state of Alaska (they financed his Columbia University education) and must do four years medical service in Cicely.

Josh Brand and John Falsey, series creators and executive producers, are best-known for their hit creation St. Elsewhere. Since creating *Northern Exposure*, they have added *I'll Fly Away* and *Going to Extremes* to their credits.

TRUE INSPIRATION

The inspiration for *Northern Exposure* came in part from a friend of the producers who was practicing medicine in rural upstate New York and from stories of medical students who would accept inner-city or rural posts in exchange for payment of their medical training. With this novel idea in hand, they chose the exotic location of the Alaskan wilds. According to the producers, "it represented a place where people could express their individuality. People could go there to create themselves. There's more than meets the eye to almost everyone in Cicely."

Filmed outside Seattle, Washington in the towns of Redmond and Roslyn (est. pop. 850), *Northern Exposure* creates its own remote Alaskan town of Cicely (pop. 839). Deep in the snow-filled mountain terrain, the small towns effectively captures the idiosyncrasies of Cicely.

The local townsfolk also add to the texture of the series. Benefitting from the contacts established by a local casting agency, *Northern Exposure* employs a high concentration of Native Americans and other locals to uniquely represent the personalities found in this fictional Alaskan town. One such casting endeavor resulted in the hiring of Elaine Miles, a Native American from the Seattle area. While waiting in the casting agency's reception area for her mother (she was trying out for a part), Elaine was "discovered" and cast as Marilyn, Joel Fleishman's assistant.

"It's a woman's name,"

Joshua Brand explained about the fictional town's name. He and co-creator John Falsey both settled on it because it's not what you'd expect in rough-and-tumble Alaska. "And it's pretty. And it's delicate. And Alaska is so rugged and wild."

"Chris needs to belong," revealed John Corbett, about why his disc jockey character loves Cicely. "This town really gives him that."

In his own display of quirkiness, Corbett has a unique reason for renting hotels and not settling in a permanent home in Washington state where the series is produced. "There is something about fresh sheets," he admitted. "Those tight sheets. So tight you can't hardly wedge your feet in. There's nothing like a bed made by a professional."

"It's the conceit of the relationship that something draws them close and then keeps them apart at the last minute," explained Rob Morrow about Fleischman's love/hate relationship with O'Connell. "I think she likes his intelligence," said Turner of O'Connell's attraction to the good doctor. "He challenges her."

"We're in a mythic, bigger-than-life environment," said Corbin of the importance of location in the series' success. "They talk about the quirkiness but it's also gentle world. In many ways it's an idealized world which I think we're kinda hungry for." It's for that reason, revealed Corbin that Maurice will never see an urbanized Cicely. "You can't do it. It's like trying to put pavement on a marshmallow," he noted.

Josh Brand is a bit disturbed that there is a need to pigeonhole Northern Exposure. "In the spirit of Cicely I hope people will step outside the normal limits of comedy and drama and appreciate it as is. We have jokes in our show, but we're not really a joke-driven show. We're driven by story and character," Brand proclaimed.

"The only two things you know for sure are that he's a hermit and a highly trained chef with his finger on the pulse of the New York restaurant world," mused Adam Arkin on his slightly bizarre alter-ego, the chef Adam. "He's real out-there. Even for this show."

"You can't do [any of] this on 'Designing Women' or 'Golden Girls,'" noted production designer Woody Crocker. When he was approached to work on the show, he said, "I read a script and said 'This is special.' It's like we all went out fishin' to a mountain stream and found gold nuggets."

Ed Chigliak's wisdom is part of the town's backbone, but it isn't simplemindedness. Darren Burrows who plays Ed, said, "Joshua (Brand) came to me and said, 'We want to make sure Ed doesn't become Barney Fife—the town idiot.' He said, 'Ed has a 180 IQ. There. I've done it. Now no one can say he's dumb.' "Waking up in the morning and being allowed to live another day—that's what keeps that perpetual smile on his face. If everyone were more like Ed this'd definitely be a better place to live."

After Northern Exposure appeared, comparison with that other offbeat Northwestern series, Twin Peaks, was immediate but producer Matthew Nodella set the record straight. "We're real and they are not," he quipped. "We're not as eclectic as Twin Peaks is, but I hope we have the same audience. I appreciate their audience as well." "We don't kill anybody," said Elaine Miles, pointing out another contrast in the two series. "I don't watch Twin Peaks. I never understood it," she admitted.

The real town of Roslyn, Washington has doubled as the exteriors for fictional Cicely, but not all of Roslyn's citizens are pleased by the visitors. "Once in a while they can block the whole entire street," criticized one town resident. "It's an inconvenience." "Maybe we're getting a little tired of them," explained a waitress at the real Roslyn Cafe. "This used to be a quiet town." "They're a pain in the butt but they do help business I would say," said Jim Luster, proprietor of the real Brick tavern in Roslyn. "Here it is a movie star," Luster said of his little backwater bar.

Buildings aren't the only facet to Roslyn that is gaining prominence. Also gaining plenty of exposure on "Northern Exposure" are Native Americans. Portrayal of Natives and their culture is important to the series. "We try to stay away from stereotypical things, like Tonto or something. I like the way it was written, and it wasn't with a bad accent or stupid or anything like that," explained Darren Burrows, a Native American himself.

Elaine Miles is another series regular who is a Native on and off-screen. She feels the show is honest about the culture. "Stereotyping is if they are making you show up in buckskins and braids," she said. "We don't always have braided hair." The producers are pleased by the vital Native American element to the show. "We found a tremendous talent pool within the Indian population here," producer Nodella said.

Many of the Native American locals come in as extras on the series, earning $50 as an extra. "Basically, what we are is mugs," said on Native local. "They say, 'background,' and they are talking about us." "It doesn't require any acting classes to be Indian," quipped one Native American extra from Roslyn.

III

MOOSE MUSIC

Think of music as an unsung supporting cast.

. . . John McCullough does. He is the quirky-but-lovable show's music consultant, assigned the formidable task of tracking down long-forgotten songs and artists and securing the rights to use them for more than just background fodder.

"The fun thing with *Northern Exposure* is, it's all over the map," McCullough says in an interview from his Los Angeles-area home. "You never know what to expect from week to week."

Music plays a prominent role, setting the tone for many of the scenes. A jukebox in the town's only bar plays obscure oldies, as does the lone radio station (when the poetic disc jockey's not gossiping or reading from "War and Peace" over the air). The songs McCullough has selected, with the approval of executive producer Joshua Brand, run the gamut - from show tunes to little-known numbers by blues singers, rappers and country artists.

Apparently, viewers are listening intently, because the network receives a steady flow of letters inquiring "What was that tune playing in the bar during the final

By Gerry Galipault

scene for this season's last episode?" or, "What Nat King Cole song was that I heard in the background of last night's show?" (The answers: Etta James' 1961 hit "At Last" and Cole's bluesy "When I Grow Too Old to Dream.")

"It's just something that evolved," McCullough says of the show's wide-ranging musical tastes. "It's really (associate producer) Martin Bruestle and Joshua's influence that it has ended up in this direction. It was brought up when we first started that Josh made it clear he wanted things that aren't really well known. He wanted the songs we all call 'the gems,' that no one really knows about or perhaps doesn't remember. Like there's a cut we found by Aretha Franklin, her version of 'Somewhere Over the Rainbow,' that we're just waiting for the right spot to put it in. It's one of those ultimate cuts that gives you goosebumps all over."

Audiophiles with a mighty-keen ear may be able to detect other gems: "Downhearted," by Mildred Bailey (one of the earliest female blues singers); "It's Just a Girl Thing" by female rapper Icy J (parts of her video also appeared); the original "Louie Louie," circa 1956, by R&B great Richard Berry; several cuts by early '60s balladeers Bud & Travis, and some cajun tracks by Buckwheat Zydeco.

"One of the best uses of a song I've seen, and I'll be the first to admit it wasn't my idea," McCullough says with a laugh, "was a Lindsey Buckingham tune called 'D.W. Suite.' He wrote the song in memory of (late Beach Boys drummer) Dennis Wilson, from what I understand, and that made it difficult for us to get it because it was such a personal thing with Lindsey. The song fit perfectly with the episode, which was about the annual breaking of the ice and everybody was getting spring fever. We used it in the opening where there were shots of the ice melting, and then we used it at the end when all the men performed the ritual of running naked through the town."

McCullough has a Masters degree in music from USC and started out doing session work in L.A. He also helped with the opening ceremonies for the '84 Summer Olympics. "I figured as long as I was going to live in L.A. I might as well get involved in the music business," he says. "If I'm going to put up with the traffic, I might as well make it worthwhile.

"It pretty much went from there. I was real fortunate that I was able to get on a show called *Tour of Duty*, and everything just kind of snowballed from there. After that, *The Wonder Years* came along and it's been like a calling card for me."

From his office, McCullough juggles his time between *Northern Exposure* and *The Wonder Years*, as well as handling all the music for *The Trials of Rosie O'Neil*. "With *Northern Exposure*, usually what I do is send them a lot of tapes, saying that I think the cuts off this tape will work in these instances, rather than specific scenes. "I've been pretty lucky. With *Northern Exposure* and *Wonder Years*, I work pretty much out of my office. In other words, there isn't a lot of me having to be on the set or having to have a lot of meetings, because we do a lot of it over the phone and send tapes around."

A *Wonder Years* album containing oldies and remakes was released several years ago. McCullough jokes that "it was on the market for like a week." Though compilation albums from TV series are hard to sell, he says, they are toying with the idea of one for *Northern Exposure*.

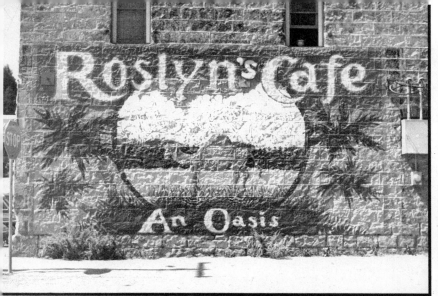

Photos by Anita J. Micuel

IV

EXPOSING THE FANS

Most successful series develop

some sort of fan following, it just depends on what form it takes. For some, it hardly exists at all, for others it's a matter of teenboppers ogling their idols. Others are far-flung, highly established, and intense, such as the Star Trek or Quantum Leap fans, with their huge conventions and other organizations.

Northern Exposure's fan phenomenon is still growing. Two known fan clubs have begun to make their mark. One, simply, is the "Northern Exposure Fan Club" in Florida, which publishes a newsletter, Northern Lights and maintains semi-official ties to the show itself. It's reasonably large at 300 plus members.

The other is slightly smaller, but no less dedicated. It is called An Oasis, "The Premier Northern Exposure Fan Club." Based in Philadelphia, it is run by a gentleman named Anthony Burokas. An Oasis can count members in several states, all of whom receive *Musings*, the club newsletter. Published "almost every month," according to Burokas, Musings contains news, letters, episode synopses and runs trivia contests with prizes. "In the newsletter, I have trivia contests that hopefully makes the viewer watch the shows more closely, trying to catch those little things that you might not catch by casually watching a show," Burokas explained.

Burokas formed An Oasis in January, 1992 to "involve the fans of Northern Exposure more than just watching the TV, which tends to involve the viewer than a lot of shows do, anyway," he noted.

Communication among fans is Burokas' primary goal. "One person wrote in asking if he could [look] for penpals," through the newsletter, Burokas remarked. He took that one step further. "Rather than solicit penpals and write to one person in particular, by having your letter in Musings and inviting replies, you can have more than one person respond to your letter and get lots of different views. It's just like a big forum on paper."

Burokas envisions it as a meeting ground for "isolated" fans. "You can share your opinions with people all across the country and get feedback," said Burokas. "I try to have a news-like section" in every issue "telling people where they can find the stars, what magazines you can find a lot of actors in."

"In the beginning, [An Oasis] was just a group of friends and it spread by word-of-mouth," Burokas remembered. "When I let the *Northern Exposure* office in Los Angeles know about us, then they forwarded a couple people to us so we had a couple people around the country. Then, we were mentioned on E! Entertainment Television and a flood of letters came in. Then the other *Northern Exposure* fan club— 'The *Northern Exposure* Fan Club' in Florida—listed us in their newsletter, and another flood of letters came in."

Membership in An Oasis costs $10, but for that you will not only get the newsletter, but Burokas' self-published *Guide* when it is finished. Burokas' *Guide* is a fan collection of actor biographies, character profiles, songlists, and a few reprinted articles from various commercial magazines. He's more than half-finished and it does show promise. "It's a comprehensive guide to the shows from the first two seasons.

"The *Guide* mostly exists in the fictional realm of Cicely. It talks about the fictional characters, and it talks what life is like in Cicely. One of the parts that I like about the book is the the incidental characters section—going through each show finding who popped in, who vanished. I'm writing little bios about these incidental characters.

While Burokas is excited about the series itself, he has been less-than-enthusiastic about the merchandising that has come with it. "The publicity they do in the form of books and calendars and the album, those things don't seem to reflect the nature of the show, which is: we present the show and you pull out of the show what you want, but we put so much in form of music and thoughts, and content, that the show is really rewarding that way The other things they've produced for marketing really don't seem to match up that way. They're just tossed at you.

"I got the calendar and there are misspellings in the calendar. They have the name of one of the [episodes] wrong. These are things I think should be checked. I think the fans having a fan club can let the fans get involved. I think the fan clubs will let the show grow" more than the commercial marketing.

"Just like *Northern Exposure*, there's a whole host of different people out there. There are people out there who joined and I never get anything from. I think they just like getting the newsletter. They're quiet, sort of like Holling. Then there are other people who just want to be doing everything and getting involved. They always write and always contribute. That's spirit of *Northern Exposure*: different people get involved in different ways. We accommodate everyone. Those who don't contribute hopefully still find interest in the newsletter, and those who do, we have find ways to make it exciting for them, as well."

Burokas feels, however, it would be impractical to expand the show's fandom beyond the scope it is right now, such as to put on a *Northern Exposure* convention of some sort. "I don't really don't have a staff here. If I had two other people with me, I suppose we could put together a big meeting of such. The other thing we run into is that there's a fan in almost every state in our fan club.

"We would either have to hold something in the center of the country or go to Roslyn and have it. That way people are walking around the town, going, 'Hey, this is what it looks like. It looks so much bigger on TV,' or something like that," he joked.

In the meantime, to write to An Oasis: P.O. Box 42433, Philadelphia PA 19101. To write to The Northern Exposure Fan Club in Florida, send to: P.O. Box 2605, Orlando FL 32802-2605.

Photos by Anita J. Micuel

THE PRODUCERS

Emmy Award-winning Joshua Brand and John Falsey are the creators of the fictional town of Cicely, Alaska and of the television series *Northern Exposure*. Having created some of television's most memorable and highly-acclaimed series including St. Elsewhere and A Year in the Life, Brand and Falsey have again pushed the envelope of network television to new limits.

"I think what's so wonderful about *Northern Exposure* is that it is character-driven," Falsey remarked. "I think in the beginning, CBS was expecting more of a [conventional] medical franchise. They would have been happy if Joel Fleishman jumped into a helicopter to rescue a lumberjack who had fallen out of a tree. We got lucky because it started in the summer and CBS wasn't paying that much attention.

"CBS kind of overlooked *Northern Exposure* that first summer. The critics looked at it and said, 'Wait a minute. This is good.' By the time CBS ordered the next episodes the following spring, there was enough trust in us for them to say: 'I guess they know what they're doing.'"

Brand agrees about the importance of characters. "European comedies are character-driven, while American comedies are joke-driven," Brand said. "I wanted to do a comedy that was gentler, more humane."

Brand, a 1972 alumnus of City College of New York with a B.A. degree in English Literature, graduated magna cum laude and was named to Phi Beta Kappa. Later, he was given a fellowship to Columbia University where he received an M.A. degree with honors in English literature in 1974.

His full-length play "Babyface" was presented at the Cast Theater in Los Angeles in 1978, and was chosen as a semi-finalist in the noted Louisville Actor Theater's Great American Play Contest. In addition, "Grunts," a full length play, has been given staged readings at the American Conservatory Theater in New York. "Grunts" was originally produced at the Wonderhorse Theater in New York in 1983.

John Falsey is a 1975 alumnus of Hampshire College with a B.A. in English. Later, he graduated from the Iowa Writer's Workshop with an MFA in Creative Writing. His short story "Bachelors" appeared in The New Yorker magazine 1978.

In 1979, Falsey joined the production staff of The White Shadow as story editor. A year later Brand also joined the series as story editor. In 1981 and 1983, they were finalists for the prestigious Humanitas Award in the 60 minute category. The team went on to create and produce the award-winning television series, St. Elsewhere. Additionally they developed Amazing Stories with Steven Spielberg and served as supervising producers for the show's first season.

Since the debut of Exposure, Brand and Falsey have turned their creative efforts to creating other series. Their show, *I'll Fly Away,* is on NBC and competed in the same category as Exposure at the 1992 Emmys. They have also created *Going To Extremes* for ABC. It's about medical students on a Caribbean island but is not a take-off on Northern Exposure. "It's very funny, the characters are offbeat, you have a clash of cultures, but it is not another *Northern Exposure*, nor was it meant to be," Falsey explained. "It's not as character-driven. It has a story-line that goes all the way through."

THE PLAYERS

Dr. Joel Fleishman

Rob Morrow portrays Dr. Joel Fleishman, the quintessential "fish out of water" in *Northern Exposure*. Joel is an inveterate New Yorker who has been reluctantly transplanted to the remote Alaskan town of Cicely. Immediately welcomed by the odd-ball locals of Cicely, the reluctant Joel struggles to operate in the sparse, make-shift medical office set up for him and has trouble accepting what passes for "normal" behavior in this eccentric little town. Morrow brings a disarming warmth to Joel's griping as he copes with his perpetual relocation angst. "I don't mind playing Joel as whiny as long as people believe he cares," Morrow has said. "We come from the same area," Morrow said of his alter ego, "and a lot of our values are the same. But he hates being stuck in the middle of nowhere. I think I'm much more open."

Born and raised in New Rochelle, NY, Morrow began pursuing a professional acting career fresh out of high school. A number of odd jobs in the theatre led to his first break. While working as an assistant to Michael Bennett on "Dream Girls," Bennett cast him for a major role in the play "Third Street" at the Circle Repertory Theater.

Among Morrow's more than 35 performances on stage are leading roles in Chaim Potok's musical adaptation of "The Chosen," Bennett's "Scandal," "Soulful Scream of the Chosen Son," "The Boys of Winter," and "Slam." His most recent theatrical performance was in the Naked Angels and subsequent Long Wharf

productions of Jon Robin Baitz's "The Substance of Fire."

Morrow made his film debut in 1986 in the comedy *Private Resort* with Johnny Depp. In addition to his leading role on the television series *Tattingers*, Morrow guest-starred in the series *Fame* and *Spencer For Hire*. However, perhaps most people remember Morrow from the elevator scene in the chewing gum commercial.

Morrow maintains his residence in New York City where he is a member of the Ensemble Studio Theater and The New York Stage and Film Company. In his spare time, he has developed a new and unlikely obsession—golf—a sport he grudgingly learned to realistically portray the golf-obsessed Dr. Fleishman.

Northern Exposure co-creator and producer John Falsey said of Morrow, "He has this very winning quality about himself—it's self depreciating, but he's nobody's schmuck."

MAGGIE O'CONNELL

Janine Turner portrays Maggie O'Connell, a beautiful, independent bush pilot and landlady to Joel Fleishman. As the primary thorn in Dr. Fleishman's side, Maggie struggles between her disdain for Joel's whiny ways and her reluctant physical attraction to him.

Born in Lincoln, Nebraska and raised in Ft. Worth, Texas, Turner began her performing career with modeling and dance and the age of three. Beginning with dance apprenticeship with the Ft. Worth Ballet in her pre-teen years, she moved easily into acting with a performance in a local theater production of "Charlotte's Web." At 15, her mother took her portfolio to the Wilhimina modeling agency and two weeks later she became their youngest client. After studying at the Professional Children's School while in New York, Turner and her parents returned to Texas.

Back in Ft. Worth, Turner was discovered by Leonard Katzman, producer of *Dallas* and was cast in a recurring role as Lucy's friend Susan. Encouraged by Katzman, Turner moved to Los Angeles after high school where she landed her first series, a late-night soap called *Behind the Screen*. Although the series lasted only 13 weeks, it drew the attention of the producers of the daytime soap *General Hospital*, who subsequently signed her to a year-long contract. During this time she did a cameo in the feature film *Young Doctors in Love*, co-starred in *Knights of the City* and portrayed Shevan Tillman in Dino De Laurentis' feature film *Tai-Pan*.

Turner was romantically involved with actor Alec Baldwin and the two were nearly married. "I had the dress and the invitations and everything," she revealed. "But we were young, at different places in our lives."

Turner moved back to New York in 1986 to hone her acting skills. She spent the next three years studying with Marcia Haufrect (a member of Lee Strasberg's Atcors Studio) and acting coach Mira Rastova. She went on to perform in several off-Broadway productions such as "Full Moon and High-Tide in the Ladies' Room" with the Ensemble Studio Theatre. When in New York, Turner is also a member of the avant-garde theatre group, The Common Ground Theatre, where only original works are performed.

Her additional film credits include co-starring roles in George Romero's *Monkey Shines*, *Steel Magnolias* as Olympia Dukakis' niece, and *The Ambulence* with Eric Roberts and James Earl Jones.

Turner resides near Seattle and maintains a residence in Texas. She enjoys horseback riding (on her horse "Maggie"), writing poetry, attending the opera and listening to classical and country music. She is not often found without her companion/dog Eclaire.

MAURICE MINNIFIELD

Barry Corbin portrays Maurice Minnifield, town patriarch of Cicely. A burly ex-astronaut and gung-ho president of the Cicely Chamber of Commerce, Maurice sees Cicely as a haven of limitless potential, soon to be the new "Alaskan Riviera." He also feels it is his duty to keep the good Dr. Fleischman practicing medicine in anticipation of Cicely's coming urbanization.

Born and raised in Dawson County, TX, Corbin has appeared in almost 100 films and television shows in the last decade. He began his performing career at Texas Tech, where he studied and performed everything from the great masters to the contemporary playwrights. After two years in the Marines, Corbin began performing in regional theater across the country for three years. He moved to New York in 1964 and during the next decade starred on Broadway, off Broadway, and in regional and dinner theaters in such roles as Henry in "Henry V," Jud in "Oklahoma," Oscar in "The Odd Couple," Henry in "Beckett," and the lead in "MacBeth."

Corbin relocated to Los Angeles in 1977, writing plays for National Public Radio when he was cast as Uncle Bob in the film *Urban Cowboy*. He also starred in other notable films including *The Man Who Loved Women*, *WarGames*, and *The Best Little Whorehouse in Texas*.

Corbin has appeared in numerous television miniseries and telepictures such as *Lonesome Dove*, *The Thorn Birds*, *Fatal Vision*, and *Young Harry Houdini*. Outside of *Exposure*, he was most recently seen in the TNT's western Conagher co-starring Katherine Ross and Sam Elliot. He has made guest appearances on such series as *Murder, She Wrote*, *Hill Street Blues*, and *Matlock*.

Corbin serves on the faculty of Texas Tech and has had seven of his original plays produced on the Pacifica Radio Network. An avid horseman, Corbin competes in celebrity rodeos. He lives in Los Angeles with his wife, two sons, and a recently discovered daughter.

ED CHIGLIAK

Darren E. Burrows portrays Ed Chigliak, a young Native American who helps Dr. Joel Fleishman (Rob Morrow) adjust to his new rural environment. Possessing an uncanny sense of timing, Ed often appears out of nowhere, spouting bits of wisdom gleaned from the many films he's seen. His unclouded, naive observations and 180 IQ lend a colorful contrast to Dr. Fleischman's inbred obstinance.

Like his character, Burrows is of Native American heritage. Born on September 12 in Winfield, Kansas, Burrows is one quarter Cherokee and a quarter Apache. After experiencing the simple pleasures of small-town life, Burrows was eager to "see the world," and went west to California.

After spending a few years searching for a career path, Burrows attempted the acting profession. He landed his first professional job in the horror film 976-EVIL after graduating from the Billy Drago/Silvana Gallardo Workshop.

He spent three months in Thailand appearing in Brian DePalma's picture, *Casualties of War* with Sean Penn and Michael J. Fox. Burrows had the role of Cherry, a naive member of the platoon. He starred in the film *Class of 1999* and in the Johnny Depp film *Cry Baby*.

On television, Burrows had a recurring role on the CBS series *TV 101* and guest-starring appearances in *Hard Time on Planet Earth* and *Dragnet*. He performed in Los Angeles theater, in productions of "Dark of the Moon" at Crown Upton Dinner Theater and "Simpson Street" at the Los Angeles Workshop.

He resides in Bellevue, Washington, and is an avid outdoorsman. He enjoys motorcycles, camping, and horseback riding. He is a big rodeo fan and has recently begun learning rope tricks.

HOLLING VINCOEUR

Tony Award-winning stage actor John Cullum plays Holling Vincoeur. A 62-year-old naturalist and adventurer, Holling has given up big game hunting to settle down as proprietor of the Brick, Cicely's local tavern. He has also settled into romantic bliss with Shelly, his 18-year-old girlfriend (Cynthia Geary)—former Miss Northwest Passage. Shelly had been brought to Cicely by Holling's best friend Maurice (Barry Corbin), but Shelly was all for Holling when they met.

Born and raised in Knoxville, Tennessee, Cullum majored in speech and English at the University of Tennessee before fulfilling his obligation as an Army reserve officer by serving a two-year term in Korea. Upon returning, he relocated to New York to pursue a professional career in the theater.

In his first Broadway show, Cullum originated the role of Sir Dinidan and acted as a stand-by for Richard Burton on Broadway in "Camelot." He received the Theatre World Award and Tony nomination for his first starring role in "On a Clear Day You Can See Forever." In 1975, he was honored with his first Tony Award for Best Actor in a Musical for his part in "Shenandoah," as well as the Drama Desk Award and the Outer Circle Critics Award. He received his second Tony in 1978 for "On the Twentieth Century."

Cullum also appeared as Laertes in Richard Burton's "Hamlet," directed by Sir John Gielgud, "The Trip Back Down," "Deathtrap," "Private Lives," with Burton and Liz Taylor, "Man of La Mancha," the role of Rutledge in the musical "1776," a part he reprised in the film adaptation. More recently, he appeared in the acclaimed "Aspects of Love"

Besides Northern Exposure, Cullum starred in the highly-rated and controversial TV movie, *The Day After* as well as *Shootdown* starring Angela Lansbury. He has directed and guest-starred in episodes of NBC's *Quantum Leap*. On the silver screen, Cullum appeared with Sissy Spacek in *Marie* and *Sweet Country* with Jane Alexander.

Cullum and his wife, Emily Frankel, an internationally renown dancer, playwright and novelist, reside in Bellevue, Washington.

CHRIS STEVEN

John Corbett plays Chris Stevens, Cicely's resident disc jockey. Known to quote Walt Whitman over the air on KBHR's "Chris In The Morning" show, as well as playing an off-the-wall musical mix ranging from jazz to showtunes to rock'n'roll, Chris provides a running commentary on the off-beat goings-on in Cicely.

Born on May 9 in Virginia, Corbett grew up in the '60s, a free-thinking liberal in middle class surroundings. Unclear about a life's career, Corbett worked six years in a steel factory until an injury forced him to redirect himself. Remembering those days, Corbett said, "It's either the coal mines or the steel factory— they're union jobs, they pay the best." Of his accident, he said, "Some pipes hit me in the back. I didn't get cut or anything....[It was like getting] hit by a car." After that he tried college, where he discovered acting.

Shortly after moving to Los Angeles, his professional career began with a series of high profile television commercials for companies such as Samsung Electronics, Foster's Beer, and DHL Courier. After appearing in dozens of commercials, Corbett landed a guest role on ABC's *Wonder Years*.

He made his film debut in the picture *Flight of the Intruder* with Willem Defoe and Danny Glover. On stage, Corbett was seen in productions of "Witness for the Prosecution," "Hair," "Under Silkwood," and "Marathon '33."

Corbett remembers his "introduction" to Chris. "They had Chris before I walked in, but I think I helped develop him. The writers really haven't spent enough time with me to know me, so it's really funny when these scripts come up, and Chris is welding sculptures or riding a Harley, which is like me. In the monologues,they let me mention my friends' names, the high school I went to. It's a fine line—where does this character start and where does John come in?"

One thing a disc jockey character would influence in the actor might be music. It's true in Corbett's case. "Musically, I tend to listen to the lower 90s on the FM tuner now—which is a lot of talk radio, a lot of jazz and opera, college stations. I don't tend to go above 95 on the radio because it just tends to be bullshit and advertisements."

Corbett currently lives near Seattle and Los Angeles, where he plays percussion in a jaz/New Age group called The Matthew Stoneman Band. He also sang for an *Exposure* cast Christmas party. "That's the most daring thing I've done because I was having a fucking heart attack. There were a couple hundred people there and a band...it was rockin'." In addition to music, Corbett plays softball, basketball, and pool.

MARILYN WHIRLWIND

Elaine Miles portrays Marilyn Whirlwind, the quiet but wise assistant to Dr. Joel Fleischman (Rob Morrow). Marilyn's subtle persistence and calm demeanor is the perfect foil to Fleischman's neurotic behavior. From the moment they meet at the doctor's makeshift office where Marilyn insists on applying for a job Joel claims doesn't exist, the doctor knows he has met his match.

Born on April 7 in Pendleton, Oregon, Miles was raised outside of the Seattle area and was a member of the Umatilla tribe, one of three tribes on her reservation. Brought up with her parents' traditional Native heritage, one half Cayuse and one half Nez Perce, Miles learned her culture through ancestral storytelling.

Skilled in the traditional activities of her tribe: beading, pottery, and weaving, Miles is also a prize-winning traditional Native dancer, winning second place in Women's Traditional Buckskin dancing at the Goodwill Games in Everett, Washington.

SHELLY TAMBO

Cynthia Geary has the part of Shelly Tambo, former teenage Miss Northwest Passage. After arriving in Cicely with Maurice Minnifield (Barry Corbin), who performed as judge at Shelly's Northwest Passage pageant, Shelly quickly dropped him in favor of his best friend, Holling Vincoeur (John Cullum).

A native of Jackson, Mississppi, Geary is the youngest of four children in what she describes as an "All-American family." Encouraged at an early age by her mother—a voice and music teacher—she studied ballet, voice, and piano while starring in all of her school's musical productions since the age of six.

Geary earned a Bachelor of Arts degree in vocal performance, graduating with honors from the University of Mississippi. While attending summer school at UCLA during her sophomore year of college, Geary was enchanted by the West Coast. After relocating to Los Angeles upon graduation, she waited tables while honing her craft. In classic Hollywood fashion, she was discovered by a talent manager who helped launch her career.

Her acting career began with a series national commercials for Coke and General Motors. She landed the lead in the play "Senior Prom" at the Off-Ramp Theatre in Los Angeles, and moved to television where she guested on the soap *The Young and the Restless*, as well as making appearances on *Divorce Court*, *Adam 12*, and *Superior Court*.

Geary currently resides near Seattle and enjoys singing and working out in her spare time.

RUTH-ANNE

Actress Peg Phillips portrays storekeeper Ruth-Anne who dispenses psychological insight along with the general goods necessary for a small town. Originally hired to take on a bit-part, the role of Ruth-Anne has grown to provide a regular base of not only comedy but human insight.

She says that she never wanted to do anything but act. After she raised her kids, and helped raise the grandchildren part of the way, she retired at the age 65. She enrolled in the drama school at the University of Washington. Today she fills the part of the sage, reliable storekeeper with ease.

JANE O'CONNELL

Jane O'Connell is mother to Maggie and a creature of habit from hot lemon juice and marmalade to her marriage of 32 years. She comes to Cicely to inform her daughter that she intends to divorce Maggie's father, Frank. Perhaps subconsciously, Jane encourages Maggie to move on in her life when she burns down Maggie's home.

Jane is portrayed by veteran Emmy-winning actress Bibi Besch. "There were a lot of people up" for that part, Besch explained in a phone interview. "I think a lot of people wanted that part. Fortunately, the audition went well enough for me to get it. They liked my take on the character. It's a very whimsical character and I played it that way, but I played it very light. It's such a light show. Light meaning 'airy.' So that's how I approached her," Besch said, remarking on her character development.

Besch saw something special in Jane that really attracted her. "I like the show very much, I think it's a really offbeat show. The character is very offbeat. I mean, she's not your usual middle-aged lady on television," Besch remarked. "Most people on television who are my age are either victims or they're bitches. They have very few redeeming qualities. She was a wonderful combination of things that I really like. I thought she was a really interesting, quirky, funny, curious likable, and charming."

If this character attracted Besch so much, was there a part of Jane that Besch is? "It's hard to separate you and your characters. She comes out of me, so I guess there's a part of me that's like that. I like that. I like her as a character."

Playing this character was an extra plus for Besch because she had been a Northern Exposure fan right along, and she got to work with some acquaintances again. She had worked with Janine Turner before and had starred with John Cullum in the ground-breaking telefilm The Day After. "I know Janine, so it was wonderful playing her mother in this. It was very easy to establish a familial relationship. It wasn't difficult to be mother and daughter. In fact, I think was easy for her two. She had be very vulnerable with me, and me with her, and that was effortless because we knew each other. It added a dimension to scenes we had together.

"So often times you're cast in parts and you have a relationship with someone: you're either married or you're their mother or daughter or whatever to this other person, and you've never met until you arrive on the set. It's a challenge to establish a relationship instantly, one that comes across on film as a relationship, but when you know someone, the relationship you already have is easily translatable to the film so you're able to touch each other, and be with each other, and look at each other from the heart as opposed to when an actor is trying to figure out who this other actor is."

Like most other actors who have worked on the series, Bibi Besch saw something very special in it. "I think the show tends to ask and answer questions about—I don't mean to be heavy about this—about what it's like to be alive. There really aren't any other shows doing that. They deal with the unanswerable aspect of life that makes like interesting and joyous, unusual, and curious. I keep using the word 'curious.' It's a very curious show. I don't mean curious in asking questions, although it does ask questions. It's whimsical.

"One of my favorite [episodes], aside from flinging the piano, which was the other aspect to [my episode] which I thought was just brilliant was when the ice breaks. Everybody's hormones go crazy. [The series deals] with that, and that's true. When spring comes, we're affected, but nobody ever talks about it. Nobody talks about the profound sadness when the leaves begin to turn. And yet they have such a tremendous impact on us."

She also very much enjoyed the location work in Roslyn, the town that doubles as Cicely. "I thought being in Roslyn was great, being up there in the mountains with the snow was wonderful. They're obviously on a hit show and they know it, so everything is wonderfully taken care of, the details and the wardrobe and the sets. The scene we did in Maurice's house; the set is so brilliant. You get a flavor of that when you watch the show, but when you're actually on it, you see what the set designer and the prop people and the set dressing people have done, it's extraordinary. It was a big pleasure."

Besch very well may experience that pleasure again. "My understanding is that there is a plan for me to come back," she admitted. "I haven't been told what I'm going to do, although I've got an idea that I want to communicate to them. I think what would really would be fun would be to fall in love with a young Frenchman on my bicycle trip in France and I come back with him to Cicely. My daughter, of course, keeps having her boyfriends die on her, so it would be another huge bone of contention between us.

"I think whatever they do to bring me back it needs to be something where I make her life miserable yet again in a way that I don't *try* to do it or *mean* to do it. It's just that I irritate the hell out of her." Irritation aside, what Besch sees as important in the citizens of Cicely is their heart. "Everyone has a huge heart, and because of that, because all of them are basically good people — even though they may not act like it all the time — that quality allows them to get along so well and to pass over the differences that might otherwise become barriers between people and barriers to having a relationship. Of course, there in this little town in Alaska snowed in all winter, so they damn well better figure a way to get along together.

"I love them all; I think they're all wonderful characters. They've all got such a huge heart. That's why audiences have fallen in love with them, because we need to have our hearts fed. Most television shows and movies don't feed the heart. That's why we feel so empty so much of the time."

BARBARA SEMANSKI

Barbara Semanski is a tough cop, whose martial mindset intrigues and then attracts Maurice. She's a character actress Diane Delano appreciates and enjoys. She returned several times as "Maurice's gal" since her debut on Northern Exposure.

"The producers—Joshua Brand and John Falsey—had specifically asked for me after seeing me on L.A. Law. I played a bailiff on the second season, kind of a tough kind of a gal with a heart of gold," in other words, just what they needed for Barbara Semanski, explained the gregarious actress.

"It was phenomenal role. The thing that makes *Northern Exposure* so special is the writing. If it ain't on the page, it ain't on the stage, you know what I'm saying?" Delano said. "Half the battle is the writing. They do a hell of a job."

The writing there is special, according to Delano, because "it's real. It's just enough left-of-center to be interesting. The characters are very likable. [The writers] go out on a limb. They take big, big risks and they pay off with the writing. As an actor, you don't have to look at a script and say, 'Oh, my God, how am I going to make this caca work?' You get a script and say, 'Oh, my God, bless you and thank you.'"

Barbara Semanski wasn't Diane Delano's first brush with life in Cicely. "When the pilot first happened, when they were first doing *Northern Exposure*, they called me in for another role, a one-shot guest starring role. Thank God I didn't get it because then they called me back for Barbara," Delano revealed.

"They set me up as a possible love interest for Maurice," Delano remembered. "I believe at the time I knew that [I] would appear on more than one. I just didn't know how many. Up-to-date now, I've done four. From what I hear, I'm going back this season, but I'm recurring so I don't know until they call me. They call me and I'm there in a heartbeat.

"It just keeps getting better and better. I love doing Barbara and I think they like having me up there. I think the public likes it too. I also do the stunt show on the Universal Studios tour. Everybody comes up to me who sees the stunt show and knows that I'm Maurice's gal. It's big time, honey. It's Hollywood!"

Delano has nothing but positives to accentuate about work on the show. "The experience is great, the cast is terrific, the crew is marvelous. You're in God's country working. It's beautiful up where they film, especially in Roslyn where Cicely is supposed to be."

And Delano loved being Maurice's gal. "It's wonderful because I get to play with his head," she said. "I get to say, 'Come here, go away. Come here, go away. Come here, go away.' I get to be this by-the-book cop, but every once in a while maybe just a [tiny bit] of vulnerability might slip through. First and foremost, she's a cop, but I don't really know. We really haven't cracked her shell yet.

"You've seen maybe just a smidge of something brewing underneath. She's could be this big ol' trollop underneath all that. I'm hoping this season they might break her down some more. They might let her have some kind of an emotion. I'd love to end up in bed with Maurice. I'd love to let her let her hair down and go to town—get wild. But I'm not the writers. They definitely have their thoughts about Barbara as they do about every member of the cast."

Besides the writing, Delano relates to Barbara. "She's very close to who I am. Physically, she's right on the money, because that's who I am. I'm a pretty big gal, and I don't take any bullshit. I'm a puppydog, but I don't take crap from anybody. As an actress, I've always had to prove that big women can be sensual and can act and [you] don't have to have tits and ass, so to speak. You can be large, you can be overweight. You can have a physicality that isn't considered gorgeous or glamorous and still be considered a serious actress and sexy or sensual.

"You can't play anything on one level as an actress or an actor. If you do, you're boring. You have to try to slip a lot of juicy stuff in, even if you're playing a big ol' steamroller, you've just got to lighten it a little bit. I have a great time with [Barbara]. She's delicious.

Delano calls Northern Exposure "a breath of fresh air" on television. "It's so different from the norm of television. It's so risky and quirky and offbeat that it's tantalizing. It grabs you. It reaches up and sucks you into it. The characters are all so different and so likable and so non-mainstream. They're left-of-center, yet people can relate to the character. It's perfect in its kookiness. It's kooky without being weird and totally off the mark."

Working on the show made Delano a convert. She hadn't seen the series until her job as Barbara. "I didn't see it until they hired me. I had auditioned for it in the very beginning and didn't get it. Then I did a lot of other things—I've probably done fifty other television episodes. So I work quite a lot on other shows as well. In the beginning I didn't see it. When I went in and auditioned for the part, then I started watching."

Delano loves the people she worked with on the series. "They love me and I love them. We get along great. We're always talking—the makeup people and the crew—they're always pulling for me to be a regular. I would love to be a regular, but for now, I have to go with what they say. Keep your fingers crossed. Maybe I can work out a deal and be a regular and be Cicely's town sheriff. That would be the greatest."

Delano also loves working in the environment of Roslyn, but sees the intricate relationship the series has with the town. "It's a fabulous little community. I think there's like 888 people who live in this little town. It's an old mining town. The locals who live there, I'm not that well-acquainted with them. When I worked there, it was 'Hello, how are you?' and whatnot.

"I know Northern Exposure has been very good to the town. They bought [the town] a firetruck. They fed 100 families at Christmas and Thanksgiving. I know it's probably very much an intrusion, but [the town's] built up their revenue probably ten times. A lot of tourists have come up, but I guess that goes with the territory. I'm sure there are some people that poo-poo it and would rather not have [the show] there, but I think the businesses like it.

"The townspeople I've [met] in the little businesses on that little strip that you see, that street, seem very happy that they're making a whole lot of money: the pizza place, the ice cream parlor, the Roslyn Cafe does a great business. They all seem happy."

Delano is obviously highly supportive and protective of the show, and she is equally vocal about last season's controversy when Rob Morrow was threatening to walk out. "I think for the viewing public who don't know what an actor goes through and they only hear, 'Oh, he wants more money, well how wrong of him to do that.' They don't know the whole story. I don't have all the details in particular. All I can say is, if you have a number one hit series and you have good people, you should bump them up pay-wise.

"You just do it in good faith in saying, 'Thanks for the fine work you do.' There's extremes: if somebody says, 'I want $200,000 an episode,' you say, 'That can't be done,' but to me, what's $40,000 from $20,000? That's nothing, absolutely nothing when you've got an enormous hit on your hands and you're making money hand-over-fist.

"Rob Morrow's good, and I'm sorry, it is a show about a doctor that's a fish-out-of-water: a New York, Jewish doctor going to Cicely, Alaska. It *is* about him. Yes, there are other characters on the show who are great, and I don't know if they'd last if they recast [Morrow's character]. I really don't. Why chance it? Everything pivots from Dr. Joel Fleischman.

"Actors go through a lot. Actors lose their privacy, first of all. You never have a private moment, especially Rob. You have interviews and you do charity functions and you talk to people and you're and you're there. So I think asking for a little more money is not out of line. [The cast] didn't make a whole lot of money to begin with, which is neither here nor there, but in relation to any other series, no he wasn't making anything."

Another bonus for Delano has been a growing friendship with Barry Corbin, her on-screen love-interest. "Barry has invited me to the Golden Boot Awards on Saturday. He's going to be presenting an award out here in California. It's an awards ceremony to honor all cowboys in film and television and theater. Pat Buttram is the honorary chairman. It's good 'ol cowboy fun. You know, Barry is a real-life cowboy.

"He's a doll. I love him. He's a man's man, but he's sweet and soft and and kind. He's got a good heart. He's a great kisser," Delano quipped. "He's got cushy, cushy lips. He's sweet, he's very charming. I love the character he plays, I love Maurice. And I love Barry, I love the actor. So, I've got it made, made in the shade."

EVE

Actress Valerie Mahaffey won a 1992 Emmy for her portrayal of Eve, the wealthy pathological hypochondriac who marries her beau Adam (Adam Arkin). Mahaffey described her original casting for the role. "'Well, you have to play opposite Adam Arkin, do you think you can be really, really mean?'" Mahaffey recalled. "I yelled at him real good and I guess he thought I was funny. That's how it went. "Apparently, they had been looking for [an actress to play] this girl for a long time. Later, I was told there was this big search. Originally, she was supposed to be Jewish. They changed their minds I guess.

Mahaffey is pleased by her work as Eve. "I got a letter from a friend of mine who I hadn't seen in years. I went to school with him and he's now a doctor. He wrote to me and said, 'I just wanted to let you know you're frightening. You're so much like my hypochondriac patients. You're great.' It was the most wonderful letter from somebody I knew. I just gave him the chills, you know?"

She wasn't sure about the character at first. "I didn't know what to do with it. There wasn't any initial, 'Oh, yes, this is how to do this,' but as soon as I got it and I realized what a great person she is, what isn't there to be attracted to? She's very sure that she's right, and that's great to play—somebody who's sure of themselves."

Valerie Mahaffey

Part of her problem may have been a lack of context. Mahaffey hadn't seen Northern Exposure before her role there. "I kept hearing about it, but this acting class was on Monday nights, so I never saw the show. I became a fan after working on it. This is wonderfully written. It's very real, but very funny and quirky and poignant, like life."

She sees a little of herself in Cicely's hypochondriac. "There's a bit of bossiness about Eve that apparently is true of me when I'm playing a game. I'm very bossy that everybody follow the rules. There's something about her that's like me. I'm not obnoxious, at least as obnoxious as her. I'm a bit of a hypochondriac, but I do always seem to have something wrong with me so I can relate. She looks a lot like me," she jokes.

Mahaffey also didn't initially know how long Eve's stay in Cicely might be. "Apparently, Adam was possibly going to be recurring, and he knew that. I didn't. I just thought it was going to be a guest part. Very soon afterwards, my agent said, 'Well, it looks like she's supposed to come back at least a couple times this season.' Which is exactly what happened."

She felt more comfortable when she did return. "I felt more at home. I thought oh, I sort of belong here when I went back the second time. It had been so much fun the first time. That sense of belonging makes you a little more relaxed. My work process is always the same, whether it's a guest part or a regular part.

"Sometimes if I was doing a scene opposite Rob, who I find very real, I would just look at him like, 'Is that a good one?' and he'd tell me yes or no. The director would too, but because I can see Rob's work all the time, I really trust his judgement. He's very professional and very too himself which I don't mind. We became friends after a while, after he had gotten to trust me.

"We had a lot of fun, especially with Adam there. We were kind of an unholy triumvirate because Adam can't look at me without laughing and Rob can't look at Adam without laughing. When the three of us are in a scene, the producers get very mad because one or the other of us breaks up. Adam said it was because he could see something in me that I get what he's doing. Who knows why Rob can't look at Adam?

"At first I was a good girl. The last time we broke up the boys were just going. It was my close-up and I was hanging on and one of the producers chided the boys, said, 'It's not fair to the crew and it's not fair to Valerie.' Then he walked off and the two of them went [mocking], 'It's not fair to Valerie,' just like two second-grade boys. Then we pulled it together and it was okay. The editor later, when he saw that scene, just said, 'What was going on? You don't have one complete take of this scene.' But I don't think they're really mad at us. We only held them up for twenty minutes."

Despite the uncontrolled hilarity breaks or perhaps because of them, Mahaffey and Adam Arkin developed a rapport. "Adam and I hit it off right away. He's so much fun it's unbelievable. It's just a gas to work with him. He's a very funny guy, very smart, and very talented. We've become friends. He can't look at me [without laughing]—he can't do the scene. I said to him, 'Adam, would it better if you acted to space, just if I wasn't here.' He said, 'You know what, could you? Could you go away?' So he did the scene to thin air."

She also likes the on-screen relationship between Adam and Eve. "I think they really love each other, but I think they're like a lot of couples who have been together for a long time, it's not usually the lovey-dovey stuff you see on TV," Mahaffey noted. "But I think there's this thing where he's allowed to say whatever he wants about her, but if anybody else says anything bad about Eve, he jumps in to her defense. I don't think she'd do the same for him, though.

Like most, she enjoys her time filming in Roslyn, but can concede that the show probably gets in the way. "I think that they thought it would be neat to have a television show there, but we hold up traffic and it's kind of a nuisance."

The actress feels that Northern Exposure's "real, but weird," and that's what draws the viewers. "I think people enjoy that. There are so many times that I'll see a situation happen in life and I'll think that nobody would believe this, but it happens in life—the strange things people do or say or that they believe. Some of the [episodes] have gotten pretty spiritual and I think people tune in to that."

Her work on the series has made a dramatic change on her life and career. "This is amazing—I'm a guest on a show that I don't know anything about and suddenly everybody knows me. They don't know what the hell my name is yet, everybody knows my face. I just got off the plane and the stewardess said, 'I'm sorry to bother you, but what was it? Was it Cheers? I said, 'Yes, I was on Cheers.' Then my husband whispered to me, 'Northern Exposure.'

THE STORIES

STARRING

Rob Morrow as Dr. Joel Fleischman

Barry Corbin as Maurice Minnifield

Janine Turner as Maggie O'Connell

John Cullum as Holling Vincoeur

Darren E. Burrows as Ed Chigliak

John Corbett as Chris Stevens

Cynthia Geary as Shelly Tambo

EPISODE GUIDE

Pilot

Guest Starring: Robert Nadir as Peter Gilliam, Art LaFleur as Walter

Co-Starring: Peg Phillips as Ruth-Anne, Grant Goodeve as Rick Pederson, Lois Foraker as Edna, Elaine Miles as Marilyn Whirl-wind

Featuring: Tom Hammond as Patient #1, Anne Gordon as Patient #2, John Aylward as Businessman, Denise Kendall as Stewardess

Written by Joshua Brand and John Falsey

Directed by Joshua Brand

The series begins with Dr. Joel Fleischman having a one-sided conversation with a businessman on a flight to Anchorage. Joel tells the man that he received a medical scholarship from the State of Alaska, in return for which he agreed to a four-year service to the state. Although a native New Yorker, Joel attempts to convince the man, as well as himself, that a four-year stay in Alaska is "definitely doable." After arriving in Anchorage, Joel meets with Peter Gilliam, who informs him that overstaffing in Anchorage has made Joel expendable, and so he is assigned to work in Cicely. Joel is upset and doubtful, but reluctantly agrees.

After a long bus ride, Joel is dropped off seemingly in the middle of nowhere. Finally, a local named Ed picks him up, and inexplicably leaves Joel with the truck and directions to Maurice Minnifield's house. Upon arrival, Joel is met by Maurice, who is obviously a former military man. He briefly tells Joel about how he arrived in Cicely twenty years earlier, and single-handedly began developing the town into a tourist spot, and requested a "Jew doctor" as part of his development plan.

Joel is less than impressed when he finally sees the town. In his run-down office, he meets Marilyn, who wants a job as his secretary. Another of his many fits of anger and frustration sends him to The Brick, a local bar, where he calls Gilliam from a pay phone and tells him that he wants out of the contract. Gilliam informs Joel that if he backs out, he has to repay the 125,000 dollars given to him by the State of Alaska. In a panic, Joel calls his fiancee Elaine back in New York, and asks her to look for some sort of loophole in his contract.

Events begin to pick up as Joel meets several more of the town's residents. Holling, the proprietor of the bar, offers Joel something to eat while he's waiting for Elaine to call back. Holling tells Joel how he and Maurice had a falling-out over Shelly, who is both waitress and Holling's love interest. Joel, whose personality so far has been antagonistic, warms a bit to Holling. However his anger returns when he meets Maggie, who he mistakes for a hooker, but who is actually his landlord. She escorts him up to his cabin, where he sleeps a fitful night after hearing rats.

The next morning, Joel jogs seven miles into town, and stops off at Ruth-Anne's store for some water and beef jerky. In his office, several patients are waiting, as well as Marilyn, who is acting as receptionist, despite repeated explanations that there is no job. Several unusual patients are followed by a man who has been shot by his wife. A sense of eccentricity of the townspeople is seen in this cross-section of patients. Later that night, Joel is talking with Maggie in The Brick, and Maggie tells Joel about the graduate student with whom she came out to Alaska. Joel, who has had a bit too much to drink, gets sick, and wakes up in a bed at Maggie's cabin. Outside, he meets Rick, who is apparently Maggie's boyfriend and housemate.

Back at the office, Joel finds Walter, who has been stabbed by his wife. In an otherwise uneventful episode, Joel helps Walter and his wife Edna talk out their marital problems. Later that day, Elaine calls Joel and tells him that there is no way out of his contract. Joel finally resigns himself to his fate, after one final fit of rage.

At the Arrowhead Country Wonderland Festival, Joel gets a taste of the local culture, and Maurice and Holling rekindle their friendship. The episode ends rather abruptly, and has the disadvantage of having to set up the entire premise of the series, in place of any real plot. However, the introductory character interactions and background information set the tone for the series.

"Brains, Know-How, and Native Intelligence"

Guest Starring: Frank Sotonoma Salsedo as Anku

Co-Starring: Grant Goodeve as Rick Pederson, Peg Phillips as Ruth-Anne, Elaine Miles as Marilyn Whirlwind

Featuring: Armenia Miles as Mrs. Anku, Leslie Rueschenberg as Mindy, Hannah Johnson as Woman #1, Sandra DeJong as Woman #2, Jan Poore as Shirley, Mitch Hale as Man #1, Ken Schneider as Man #2, Gary Taylor as Man #3

Written by Stuart Stevens

Directed by Peter O'Fallon

The citizens of Cicely are greeted over the radio waves by Chris Stevens, otherwise known as 'Chris In The Morning', the local DJ, who has chosen to read the complete works of Walt Whitman. At the same time, Joel awakens in his cabin to find Ed in his room, wanting to make an appointment for his uncle. Joel waves him off, and proceeds to the bathroom, where he discovers that his toilet is broken. Later that morning, he complains to his landlord Maggie about the problem, but she dismisses him as a helpless whiner. As Chris continues his readings, he mentions Whitman's homosexual tendencies, which upsets Maurice. Maurice storms in from his fishing and throws Chris off the air.

Later in the day, Ed is out in the forest with his uncle, who missed his appointment with Joel. Unable to convince his uncle Anku to see the doctor, Ed tries to convince Joel to make a house call, but Joel refuses on principle. At Joel's cabin in the evening, Maggie fixes Joel's toilet on her way out on a date. In her arguments with Joel, where she calls him a "helplessness junkie," we see the first signs of the recurring conflict between Maggie and Joel as Maggie sees Joel as a spoiled, self-centered, egomaniacal New Yorker, and Joel views Maggie as an adversarial backwoods pilot with a strong masculine streak. However, this antagonism hides an underlying attraction, which is only apparent when one of the two lets their guard down, which is rare.

ANSWERS ON PAGE 149

TRIVIA TEASERS: JOEL

1) Where is Joel from?

2) Where did Joel live in NY?

3) Where did Joel graduate from?

4) Where did Joel do his residency?

5) What are Joel's parents' names?

6) Who did Joel play doctor with in the second grade?

7) Where did Joel go to camp in the summer of '78?

8) Where did Joel go to high school?

9) Where is Joel's grandmother from?

10) Who started the Fleischmans in Flushing?

11) What is Joel's grandmother's name?

12) What was Joel's great-grandfather's name?

13) Who was Joel name after?

14) What is Joel's Indian name?

15) What was Joel's fiancee's name?

16) Where is Elaine from?

17) Where did Elaine attend law school?

18) What are Elaine's parents' names?

19) What is Elaine's uncle's name?

20) When Joel is waiting to hear from Elaine in the first episode, who was the call for?

21) What does Elaine bring Joel from New York?

22) What song does Chris dedicate to Joel the day that Elaine arrives?

23) What song does Ed dedicate to Elaine?

24) Who did Elaine leave Joel for?

25) How long did Joel and Elaine date?

26) What was Joel's nickname in junior high?

27) How old was Joel when he applied for Harvard?

28) Did he get in to Harvard?

29) What was the only pet Joel ever had?

On KBHR, the local radio station, Maurice is acting DJ, following the firing of Chris. Maurice speaks out against Chris' mention of Whitman's homosexuality, and then plays music from 'Kiss Me Kate' by Cole Porter, who was ironically also a homosexual. Joel hears the broadcast from within his shower, when suddenly the water turns cold, and the handle breaks off in his hand.

In another idyllic moment, Joel visits Chris out at his trailer on the lake, ostensibly to examine his forehead, which was injured when Maurice threw him through the window of the radio station. Joel is surprised to meet Chris' sleep-over, a young lady named Mindy, and we begin to see Chris' open attitude toward sex. Feigning casual conversation, Joel asks Chris about fixing his shower, but Chris pleads ignorance, since he bathes in the lake.

In town, Joel visits Ruth-Anne's general store, which also serves as the town library. Maggie finds him looking for books on plumbing, and hassles him about his toilet. In a casual joke about Maggie's attraction to him, Joel touches on the sexual tension between them, which provokes a violent response from Maggie. After a half-hearted attempt to fix his shower with Ed, Joel finds himself at Mrs. Anku's home, having Kentucky Fried Chicken for dinner with Anku and Ed. Later in the sauna, Anku claims that he doesn't need medical help, since the body is a self-healing organism. Joel's self-centeredness falls away, and his emotional side shows through as he pleads with Anku to seek medical treatment. Anku declines, but offers Joel metaphysical advice on fixing his shower.

The next morning, Ed convinces Joel to visit Anku again, and Joel reluctantly agrees. In his office, Maggie waits with a hurt knee, which she threw out when dancing. After teasing her about her injury, Maggie storms out, enraged, and Joel smugly knows that he has bested her. That night, Joel visits Anku again, but is distracted from making a diagnosis by Anku's lesson in native dance. Joel later returns to Anku's place, and tells him that he will die if he is not treated, pleading with him to sacrifice his pride for his own health. Anku finally relents, and goes to see a specialist in Anchorage.

A town meeting is held to discuss the firing of Chris, led by Holling, who we find is also the town mayor. Maurice goes to speak, but is booed by people who are sick of show tunes. Maurice, the owner of the radio station, refuses to rehire Chris. Later, he discusses his decision with Joel, and Joel tells him that he's no good on the radio. As a result, Maurice agrees to swallow his pride and rehire Chris.

As the show closes, Joel shows up at Maggie's place at about 11 as00 at night, with medicine for her knee. In a touching moment, we see Joel completely vulnerable, telling Maggie that he's homesick. Maggie agrees to come by the next day and look at the shower, and Joel does a little dance as he walks out to his truck.

"Soapy Sanderson"

Guest Starring: John McLiam as Soapy Sanderson, Christa Miller as Laurie Batton, Darryl Fong as Kim Chang

Co-Starring: Elaine Miles as Marilyn

Featuring: Phil Lucas as William Casebear (Accountant), Nick Ramus as Chief, John Murray as Surveyor

Teleplay by Karen Hall

Story by Karen Hall and Jerry Stahl

Directed by Stephen Cragg

Early in the morning, Maggie lands her plane outside a cabin near the woods. She picks up Soapy Sanderson, an elderly man who lives alone with a team of dogs. There is an obvious closeness between Soapy and Maggie. Maggie brings Soapy in to Joel's office, and Joel is upset that they are several hours late. In addition, Joel is bothered to find that Soapy hasn't been doing his therapy for his broken hip, which is not healing very quickly.

After Joel tells Soapy to think about his future, Soapy leaves, a bit more somber than before. Later that day, Ed delivers a note from Soapy, telling Joel and Maggie to meet him at his cabin the next morning. When they arrive, they find Soapy's body, along with a gun, a will, a nice bottle of wine, and an urn for his ashes. Joel is visibly shaken, but Maggie accepts Soapy's death as part of life's cycle.

At the Brick, Holling reads the will, and Joel and Maggie are shocked to find that they have been named co-executors to Soapy's estate. Joel is especially confused, since he barely knew the man. At the bar, Joel suspiciously interrogates Maggie about the reason, and Maggie accuses him of being paranoid.

At Joel's office, a local chief shows up and offers to buy Soapy's land from Joel for $50,000, in order to use it as a tax write-off. Hoping to use the money to help shorten his sentence in Cicely, Joel tentatively accepts the offer, provided he can convince Maggie to agree. He meets Maggie later in the Brick, and rather duplicitously tries to convince her to give the land back to the Indians. Maggie hesitantly agrees, and is actually impressed with Joel for coming up with such an original idea.

Ed drives two strangers into town, who have arrived to make a documentary. At the same time, Joel is in his office talking to Elaine, and tells her to get an expensive attorney to get him out of his contract. However, he is interrupted by Maggie, who introduces him to Laurie and Kim, the two film-makers who are shooting a documentary on Soapy's life. Joel is a little uncomfortable with the attention, and begins feeling guilt over his decision to sell the land. Meanwhile, Maggie is beaming, and has apparently overcome her previous dislike of Joel.

In the evening, Maggie stops by Joel's place with dinner and wine to celebrate their decision. Joel, who hasn't told Maggie about the money, is a little nervous, but invites her in. The attraction between Maggie and Joel heightens as they pour the wine, and as they finish off the bottle in front of the fireplace, Maggie apologizes for misjudging Joel. Joel's discomfort grows, and as he tries to tell her about the money, she begins hitting on him. Suddenly, Maggie realizes what she is doing, becomes very uncomfortable, and starts to leave. Joel, who is by now thoroughly confused, asks her what is going on. Maggie admits that she was hitting on him, kisses him on the cheek, and leaves, while Joel stands alone, flustered and confused.

In the Brick, Laurie and Kim are filming footage of townspeople who knew Soapy. When interviewing Maggie, Laurie shows her a picture of Holling's dead wife, who looked exactly like Maggie. Maggie starts with the realization that Soapy's affection for her could have been related to the love of his deceased wife. Later, on a walk with Holling, Maggie brings up her past relationships, and the fact that every man she has ever gone out with ends up dead. Holling explains that maybe she is simply putting something out into the universe. Unfortunately, their conversation is cut short as Maggie spots workmen surveying the land to prepare for drilling. Her anger escalates as she realizes who is responsible.

Laurie and Kim are filming Joel in his office, when Maggie storms in an accuses him of selling out the land for his own benefit. Joel chases after her, and tries to defend himself, but Maggie remains unconvinced. As Joel stops by KBHR to talk with Chris, Chris tells him to make the best of wherever he is, a possibility that Joel had not yet considered. For the first time, he ponders accepting his place in Cicely, instead of rejecting it out of hand. He goes to patch things up with Maggie, and Maggie pours out her feelings about Soapy, and her connection with his dead wife.

They resolve their disagreements and Joel agrees not to sell the land. They fly over the peaks to drop Soapy's ashes, which end up blowing back in the cockpit. Through all the arguments, they have emerged slightly closer than before.

"Dreams"

Guest Starring: Lenny Imamura as Chiba, Michael Paul Chan as Masuto

Co-Starring: Elaine Miles as Marilyn, Grant Goodeve as Rick Pederson, Peg Phillips as Ruth-Anne, Anthony Curry as Gorman Tambo

Featuring: William Douglas Smith as Bar Patron

In an effort to expand the tourist trade of Cicely, Maurice drives in two Japanese investors in his convertible Cadillac. During the trip, he is espousing the virtues of Alaska, and Cicely in general, to Masuto, who speaks no English, and Chiba, who acts as a translator. However, the ride causes Masuto to get sick, and Maurice takes him to see Dr. Fleischman.

In Joel's office, Shelly is being examined for sickness. Since she missed her last two periods, she took a home pregnancy test, and discovered that she is pregnant. However, the examination is cut short as Maurice rushes Masuto in. Maurice tells Joel of their plan to build hotels and golf courses in Cicely, and Joel offers his services as an on-call physician, in exchange for the opportunity to partake of the resort life. This business relationship between Maurice and Joel is one of the weaker plots, and is made more difficult to watch because of Maurice's inherent dislikability. Joel is seen again as a self-serving opportunist, undermining any emotional growth previously seen.

At the Brick, Maggie advises Shelly on how to tell Holling of her pregnancy, and Holling responds with shock, but decides to propose so that the child will have a father. Maurice hears of the proposal, and the pregnancy, and his old jealousy is renewed. Later that evening, Maurice and Joel are entertaining Chiba and Masuto at Maurice's house, but Maurice begins agonizing over Shelly, and unintentionally insults the Japanese investors by his blunt comments. Joel desperately attempts to salvage the evening and finally finds common ground with the investors as golf.

The next day, Ed and his friends are laying out astroturf in a field, to create a makeshift golf course. Maggie shows up, visibly upset at the artificiality of the course, but Joel ignores her, lost in thoughts of 9-irons and doglegs. Maggie informs Joel that since he is Shelly's obstetrician, she has picked him to be the best man. Maggie herself has been named maid of honor, and Chris will perform the ceremony (he became ordained by answering a classified in the back of Rolling Stone).

At the wedding ceremony the following day, not only does Maurice not show up, but neither does Holling. Maggie yells at Joel for not keeping track of Holling, but Shelly accepts his absence as a sign that he doesn't want to marry her, and runs off. On the following day, Holling shows up at the Brick in his hunting outfit, and Shelly starts throwing glasses at him. Holling eventually ends up in Joel's office with a cut above his right eye, and explains to Joel how the men in his family have always lived over one hundred years, while their wives have always died early. As a result, he never wanted to marry, fearing that his wife would die earlier as a result. Joel convinces Holling to explain this to Shelly, and the wedding is rescheduled.

Shelly shows up at Maurice's house later that night. Although she came to try to convince Maurice to sing at the wedding, he thinks that she showed up to take him back. He begins coming on to her, and Shelly is insulted. Maurice finally kicks Shelly out. Immediately after, Chiba and Masuto prepare to leave. As Maurice stands dazed at this turn of events, Masuto speaks in perfect English, telling him to sing at the wedding. The investors depart, and Maurice is left alone.

At the wedding, Maggie and Joel are having their usual arguments, and Maurice is singing, a little grudgingly. As Chris is about to close the ceremony, Holling pulls Shelly outside, saying that he loves her, but doesn't want to marry her, because of his ancestors' luck with women. Shelly agrees, and they kiss and leave.

That night Joel is in his office away from the wedding celebration. Maurice tells him that the investment deal is off, the golf course is starting to mildew, and then leaves. Joel, having been interrupted just moments earlier, tries to call Elaine back, but gets only her answering machine. This is the first sign that something may be wrong back in New York. The ending is rather bleak, as is the episode as a whole.

"Russian Flu"

Guest Starring: Jessica Lundy as Elaine Schulman

Co-Starring: , Elaine Miles as Marilyn Whirlwind, Peg Phillips as Ruth-Anne

Written by David Assael

Directed by David Carson

Joel awakens cheerfully to Chris In The Morning playing "Who Put The Bomp", which is dedicated to Joel. As Joel gets dressed, Chris explains that Joel's fiancee Elaine is flying in today to visit, and Joel in understandably excited. In the office, Joel advises "Red" Murphy not to go up in a plane because of his sickness, not realizing that Red was supposed to fly Elaine in. In a panic, Joel finally asks Maggie to fly his fiancee in, and Maggie agrees, after charging him double.

Maggie flies in with Elaine, and Joel is waiting impatiently. As Joel helps unload her luggage, he discovers that apparently Maggie and Elaine have hit it off, and is a little disturbed, since he doesn't want his fiancee associating with someone who he dislikes as much as Maggie. However, his mood is quickly swayed by Elaine's affection. Back at Joel's cabin, they begin kissing, but are interrupted as Ed casually walks in. He tells Joel that Maurice and Chris are both sick, so Joel rushes into town, leaving Elaine to have dinner with Maggie.

As Joel enters his office the next day, he is greeted by bunches of sick people. Joel attempts to phone around to find a cure for the epidemic, when he suddenly discovers a terrible smell. Out in his waiting room, he finds Marilyn administering a tribal remedy called Hio Ipsanio, which smells like moose dung. Joel gives Marilyn a speech about administering medicine, and eventually finds his way back home, where Maggie has repaired Joel's air-conditioner for Elaine. Again, Joel and Elaine begin their romantic pursuits, but Ed interrupts, saying that Joel is needed for a town meeting to decide what to do about the epidemic. Everyone in town is angry at Joel for not curing them, and when Joel finally returns home, exhausted, he finds Elaine sick in bed.

The next morning, Elaine is crying because she feels so terrible about being sick, and points out that Joel and Maggie are the only two people in town who haven't gotten sick. Elaine also brings up the time that Maggie was hitting on Joel, and Joel felt uncomfortable (from the "Soapy Sanderson" episode). Joel thinks that Maggie told Elaine about that night to undermine their relationship, and Elaine defends Maggie. The closeness between Joel and Elaine begins falling apart, as they spend more and more of their time arguing about Maggie. Elaine begins to see the same bad qualities in Joel that Maggie always mentions.

Back in town, all of Joel's patients are gone, since Marilyn administered her remedy to everyone. Joel finally gives in, and uses some on Elaine. As they sleep that night, Joel has a dream that he is back in New York, running into various people from Cicely. When he returns to his apartment, he finds that Elaine is actually his sister, and in the dream, Maggie is his wife. After a passionate seduction by Maggie, Joel wakes up next to Elaine feeling guiltily.

The next morning, Elaine is well again, and Joel apologizes for his sudden impotence the night before. They go to town, where everyone at the Brick is friendly to Joel, in contrast to the other night when they wanted to kill him. Joel is still suspicious, and Elaine criticizes him for never cutting anyone any slack. Holling then shows up to take Joel and Elaine on a trip to see the waterfall.

The scene is filmed very similarly to "Twin Peaks," and contains many inside jokes referring to that show. The scene ends with Joel and Elaine saying goodbye as Red prepares to take off. They depart with much regret, and there is a sense that something has changed between them, that something has died. Joel returns home that night, and is deathly sick. Maggie shows up with some of Marilyn's Hio Hio Ipsanio for him, says a few kind words, and leaves.

"Sex, Lies, and Ed's Tape"

Guest Starring: Brandon Douglas as Wayne Jones

Co-Starring: Elaine Miles as Marilyn Whirlwind, Peg Phillips as Ruth-Anne

Featuring: Jeffrey Carpentier as M.C.

Written by Joshua Brand and John Falsey

Directed by Sandy Smolan

Inspired by the visiting filmmakers from a previous episode, Ed is working on a movie idea. While watching Maurice yelling at Chris, he imagines them in a scene from an Indiana Jones film. However, he soon finds that he has writer's block.

In Holling's bar, a young man shows up, looking for Shelly. He tells Shelly that he drove 600 miles to see her, and wants to marry Cindy, one of Shelly's friends from back home. Shelly is upset and asks why he needs her permission. Wayne responds that before he can marry Cindy, he has to divorce Shelly. Holling hears this, and is stunned.

In Joel's office, Rick is being given a physical. Joel finds a small growth on his chest, causing Rick to become extremely agitated. He brings up the fact that all of Maggie's previous boyfriends have died, as a result of the 'O'Connell Curse.' Joel is a little confused at his paranoia, but agrees to remove the growth and have it analyzed.

Back at the Brick, Holling is upset at finding out about Shelly's husband. Shelly tries to pass it off as no big deal, but Holling refuses to live in sin, and thinks that they should separate. Shelly is hurt by this decision, but has no choice. The next day, Rick and Maggie are in Joel's office getting advice on Rick's tumor. Joel tries to reassure them that the odds are high that the growth is not malignant, but Rick is not very accepting. Meanwhile, Maggie is continually seeking reassurance, and is trying to convince Rick that there is nothing to worry about. Clearly, Rick is living in fear.

Later, Holling and Shelly are in Joel's office, and Joel tells them that Shelly is not actually pregnant. Shelly accepts this, since she doesn't want a baby now that Holling isn't sure whether he loves her anymore. She stomps out, and Holling is left in a wake of confusion. That night Shelly is setting up a bed at Maggie's and they talk about men. Maggie confides that Rick has left town, not on business, but out of fear of her. She is clearly bothered by his behavior.

Wayne shows up to talk to Shelly, deciding to take her back. Shelly refuses, but considers the option, since Holling kicked her out. The next day, Shelly and Wayne are dancing at the Brick to make Holling jealous, and Holling suddenly gets a crick in his neck. At Joel's office, Holling asks Joel's advice. Joel tells Holling that he should have stuck by her. Finally, Shelly tells Wayne to leave, and after an abject apology, decides to take Holling back.

Maggie and Rick are in Joel's office, waiting for the results of the biopsy. Both of them are desperately trying to reassure themselves that everything will be okay, and that they will emerge from this hardship stronger than ever before. When the results come in, the tumor is found to be benign, and after a hug, Maggie tells Rick to get out, since he ran away before.

At the Indian talent show that night, Joel tries asking Maggie about Rick, and she is unresponsive. The show ends with the two of them watching Marilyn's dance for the talent show, and Ed working on his movie, his writer's block finally gone.

ANSWERS ON PAGE 149

TRIVIA TEASERS: JOEL/CICELY

1) How many scholarship applications did Joel submit?

2) How many rejections did he receive?

3) Who financed his education?

4) How much was the scholarship?

5) In return for his scholarship, how long does Joel have to serve the State of Alaska?

6) Who is Joel's contact with the State of Alaska?

7) When does Joel have to renew his Cicely library card?

"Kodiak"

Guest Starring: Elaine Miles as Marilyn Whirlwind

Featuring: Teri Thomas as Nancy, Kellee Bradley as Sue-Ellen, Wayne Waterman as Mike, Lisa Budak as Phyllis, Elise Nelson as Kerry

Written by Steve Wasserman and Jessica Klein

Directed by Max Tash

As the morning starts off, Joel receives a call from Pete Gilliam, who assigns him to teach a hygiene class in Boswell. At the same time, two military men arrive at Maurice's office in town, to inform him that his brother Malcolm is dead. Maurice accepts the news with a quiet sadness. In the Brick, at about mid-morning, Joel asks Maggie to fly him to Boswell to teach the hygiene class. Suddenly, Ed enters, and tells Holling that Jessie's back. Shelly discovers that Jessie is a bear that attacked Holling years earlier, and they've had a rivalry ever since. Holling leaves to begin packing his gear for the hunt, and Ed follows.

In Boswell, Joel and Maggie show up to the hygiene class, only to discover that it is actually a prepared childbirth class. Joel gives them four words that they need to know to prepare themselves as "I want my epidermal!" Back in Cicely, Maggie tells Joel that he is teaching the class wrong, the women should be preparing for childbirth instead of resorting to risky drugs. As a result, Maggie teaches the next childbirth class, while Joel sits cynically by.

As Holling finishes packing, Shelly decides that she wants to come along. Holling warns her of the risks, but she is willing to accompany them anyway. When they arrive and set up camp, Shelly and Holling immediately begin fooling around in the tent while Ed cooks a hot dog.

In his office, Maurice decides that he needs an heir to his fortune, and offers Chris the opportunity, since both of his parents are dead. Chris decides to give it a try, and has dinner at Maurice's that night. However, the distance of the table reflects the difference in the personalities; Maurice is a military man, while Chris is an ex-convict. Maurice tries to warm Chris to him, and gives him money to go out with, but Chris is uncomfortable with the whole situation, and even suffers impotence as a result. Finally, as Maurice is trying to teach Chris croquet, Chris becomes frustrated and walks off, relinquishing his place in Maurice's will.

In the woods the next morning, Ed is preparing to pack up camp and go after Jessie, but Holling and Shelly are still messing around in the tent. Ed finally sits back down and waits for them. Once or twice, Holling comes out of the tent, and acts like he's preparing to leave, but he always ends up back with Shelly. This becomes boring after a while, both for Ed and for the viewer. Eventually, Ed discovers that Jessie has left the area, and Holling is upset at having missed his chance, but it is too late.

At the childbirth class, one of the women starts going into labor, and Joel is forced to deliver a baby. On the flight back, Joel and Maggie talk about the experience, and their thoughts about kids. The entire experience ends up bringing them closer together.

Driving back from the woods, Holling and Shelly are asleep, and as Ed stops to relieve himself, he spots Jessie out in the woods. Ed tries to wake Holling up, but Jessie leaves before Ed has a chance.

That night, Maurice shows up to Joel's cabin, and tells him about what happened between he and Chris. Maurice informs Joel of his plans for the future as he plans to live forever. Joel laughs, but Maurice is dead serious. Maurice drives away, and Joel looks up as it begins to snow.

"Aurora Borealis as A Fairy Tale For Grown-Ups"

Guest Starring: Adam Arkin as Adam, Richard Cummings Jr. as Bernard, Elaine Miles as Marilyn Whilrwind

Co-starring: John Procaccino as Ranger Burns, Grant Goodeve as Rick Pederson, Peg Phillips as Ruth-Anne

Featuring: Ryan O'Neill as Adolescent Chris, Lou Hetler as Carl Jung, Sandy Miller as Mother

Written by Charles Rosin

Directed by Peter O'Fallon

In Cicely, the full moon is having a strange effect on everyone. Ruth-Anne is eating steak at 8 as00 am, Maurice is complaining about the coffee, and Ed tells Joel about Adam, the mysterious person with bare feet and a green head who wanders around the woods at night. Meanwhile, Chris has taped his morning show so that he can work on his sculpture, called Aurora Borealis, before the Northern Lights actually occur.

A stranger shows up in town on a Harley and new leathers. Ed comments that he's black, and that they don't have many strangers in town. The man introduces himself as Bernard, and goes over to the Brick, where he becomes engaged in conversation with Chris about Jung and the collective unconscious. There is a clear connection between Bernard and Chris, and they begin acting similarly.

Joel drives out to make a housecall for a forest ranger. On the way back, his truck breaks down leaving him stranded in the woods at night. He sees a large hulking figure come out of the woods, steal some things from his truck, and beckons him to follow. Reluctantly, Joel does, and finds himself in a cabin in the middle of nowhere. He tries to strike up a conversation with the man, but he simply tells Joel to shut up and sit down. He has a difficult time convincing Joel that he's Adam, the mysterious creature everybody's been talking about. Far from a wild beast, Adam is actually a superb chef, and cooks a meal that Joel is amazed at.

In town, Chris and Bernard are playing bridge against Maggie and Holling. Bernard rarely plays, and yet he and Chris win every hand, as if they're thinking alike. As they leave, they speak almost in unison, and Maggie and Holling look at each other in confusion.

Later that night, Chris has a dream about his father, and is surprised to run into Bernard in his dream, as well as Carl Jung. Bernard and Chris wake up simultaneously, and discover in conversation that not only do they have the same birthday, but they are also brothers. Their dad spent half of his time with each of their families, which explains the similarities, and the mental connection. Chris and Bernard are both blown away by this turn of events.

Back at Adam's cabin, Joel wakes up, but Adam is gone. Joel traces his way back to the truck, is able to start it again, and drives back home. However, when he tries to tell everyone about it the next morning, no one believes him. Everyone thinks that the moon has made him crazy.

Following the formal presentation of Chris' sculpture, Bernard and Chris say goodbye, and Bernard rides off once again into the great unknown. Joel leads Maggie and Ed back out into the woods, only to find that Adam's cabin is gone. All that is left is a garlic press, which Joel is overjoyed to find.

"Goodbye To All That"

Guest Starring: Beverly Leech as Tori Gould

Co-Starring as: Grant Goodeve as Rick Pederson, Peg Phillips as Ruth-Anne, Grant Gelt as Kid Joel, Therese Xavier Tinling as Alison, Margaret Mason as Proprietor

Written by Robin Green

Directed by Stuart Margolin

Chris In The Morning starts the day with an announcement that, after being in Cicely for eight months, Dr. Joel Fleischman is finally getting a two-week vacation to New York. Joel is working in his office, obviously excited about the trip, but is shocked when he receives a "Dear Joel" letter from Elaine, his fiancee. She tells him that she got married to Dwight, a retired federal judge from Louisville. After reading the letter, Joel leaves the office in stunned silence. Later, Ed shows up at Joel's cabin, where Joel is busily cleaning house. Ed shows concern over Joel's condition, but Joel is acting as if nothing's wrong, trying to convince himself that there are plenty of available women.

At the Brick, Holling presents Shelly with a satellite dish for the bar. Shelly is thrilled at the idea of finally being able to see the world from her own home. Later, the denizens of the Brick gather around the television, and Shelly is mesmerized by an Italian documentary. She is slowly drifting away from reality.

The next day, Joel drops by KBHR to talk to Chris. Joel asks Chris if he knows any girls around to date. Chris invites Joel to come along on a double date, and Joel jumps at the chance. Joel changes from a serious, egotistical doctor, to a more vulnerable, occasionally obnoxious young man. The change itself is entertaining, as Joel is seen try to impress the ladies with his pool prowess at the Brick later that night. Maggie expresses her sympathy to Joel about Elaine, and then notes that it hasn't taken him long to get back into the dating scene, showing at least a bit of jealousy and disappointment.

Later, Joel is really trying to impress his date with his conversation, and asks her to dance. She rejects his advances, saying, "I didn't come five thousand miles to get all sweaty with a guy who could be in my Chem class." Just as she leaves, Maggie walks by with Rick, noticing smugly that Joel is once again alone.

Shelly comes downstairs into the Brick in a formal evening gown, much to Holling's surprise. However, she is dressed up to watch Wheel of Fortune, and chides Holling for not being a fan. Later that night, Holling overhears her ordering things from the Home Shopping Network, and switching channels endlessly. She is obviously becoming more run-down and pale, but her deterioration is more sad than funny.

Late at night, Joel falls asleep alone in the movie theater. He wakes up when the projector begins running, and talks to images of an ex-girlfriend, as well as his younger self, who tells him to get over his depression. Dream sequences such as this are *Northern Exposure* trademarks, and afford an opportunity to look inside Joel's head.

The next several days show Joel sinking deeper and deeper into his depression. He has visions of showing up at Elaine's wedding, in a dream sequence similar to The Graduate. Ed wants to help him, and Joel explains that there is no closure to the whole relationship. Ed takes this as a challenge upon himself, and recruits Holling and Maggie to help Joel.

At the Brick, when all of Shelly's merchandise arrives, Holling issues an ultimatum to Shelly to turn off the television or leave. When Shelly is unable to shut it off, she flees and seeks out Chris to take her confession. With his help, she overcomes her addiction, and returns to Holling's waiting arms.

Ed shows up at Joel's cabin, and brings him into town, where a table is set up outside the Brick, recreating the circumstances of Joel and Elaine's favorite date. Holling serves iced coffee, and Maggie acts in Elaine's place, to allow Joel to vent his feelings towards her. His discussion of sex causes Maggie to break out in a sweat, but in the end, Joel achieves closure, and he and Maggie enter the Brick together.

"The Big Kiss"

Co-Starring: Peg Phillips as Ruth-Anne, Eloy Casados as Smith, Geraldine Keams as Great Aunt, Jessica Cardinahl as Girl

Featuring: Albert J. Hood as Bingo Caller, Carolyn Byrne as Mrs. Emerson, David J. Guppy as Townsperson 1, Don Eastman as Townsperson 2, Rosetta Pintado, Katherine Davis, Susan Morales, Oscar Kawagley as Bingo Players

Written by Henry Bromell

Directed by Sandy Smolan

As Chris In The Morning espouses the virtues of true love, a beautiful woman stops in and asks him for directions to Route 1. Chris is surprised, and after she leaves, he finds that he can no longer speak. He rushes in to see Dr. Fleischman, who cannot believe that he lost his voice because of a beautiful woman.

After being reminded of his lost parents, Ed wakes up to find the spirit, One-Who-Waits, in his bedroom. The spirit wants to help him find his parents, and the two of them set off the next morning on their quest. Ed shows the spirit around town, and discovers that One-Who-Waits is invisible to the white man. At the Brick, the two of them have lunch, and One-Who-Waits tells Chris, through Ed, that to regain his voice, he must find the most beautiful girl in town, and sleep with her. Maurice tells Chris of a similar Arthurian legend, and as Chris ponders this advice, Maggie walks in. Chris finds out that Rick is out of town, and stares at Maggie in wonderment.

The next night, Maggie shows up to the radio station to fix the heater, only to find that Chris has prepared a meal for her. Through note cards, he tells her that she is the most beautiful woman in Cicely, and she is very flattered, and obviously attracted to Chris. When Maggie later tells Joel of the interesting evening she had, Joel tells her of Chris' plot to sleep with the most beautiful woman in town. But instead of being angry at Chris, Maggie lashes out at Joel, who thinks that she doesn't have what it takes to give Chris his voice back. Maggie is very defensive and considers it a challenge to give Chris his voice back.

One night later, Chris shows up at Maggie's cabin to find it surrounded by townspeople who are there to see if Chris gets his voice back. Joel is among them, and is shocked that so many people have showed up for the event. Maggie answers the door in a sultry dress, Chris is obviously nervous, and Maggie ends up backing out. However, she convinces Chris that by kissing him, she can give him his voice back. He stumbles out minutes later, takes a breath,

and says, "Wow." Joel is aghast, thinking that they slept together. Later, at the radio station, Joel attempts to find out whether or not they really slept together, but Chris keeps quiet about the event, and Joel leaves a little jealous.

The spirit is unable to help Ed find his parents, and Ed bids him farewell. However, when driving home, Ed stops to help a man fix his tire. The man introduces himself as Smith, and it is only after Ed leaves that he realizes that the man is in fact his father. He smiles to himself, and drives off.

"All Is Vanity"

Guest Starring: John McCann as Frank O'Connell

Co-Starring: Peg Phillips as Ruth-Anne, Rex Linn as Martin

Featuring: Sharon Collar as Wife, O. C. "Mac" McCallum as Husband, Cathy Bryan as Patient #10, Peter Bradshaw as Man #1, Charles Russo as Man #2

Written by Diane Frolov and Andrew Schneider

Directed by Nick Marck

After Holling impresses Shelly by throwing a man out of the bar, the two of them go up to bed. Afterwards, Shelly makes an off-hand comment about Holling's uncircumcised penis, and Holling is a bit uncomfortable at the comment. He eventually goes in to see Joel, and wants to be circumcised. Joel advises against the surgery, and Holling changes his mind. Upon returning to his waiting room, Joel discovers that one of the patients is dead.

Maggie receives her mail at Ruth-Anne's store, and discovers that her father is coming by to visit that day. She hurriedly goes to pick him up, dressed in uncharacteristic pink hat and mittens. Her father arrives, and it is quickly apparent that she is daddy's little girl. Her entire demeanor changes from a self-sufficient, independent young woman, to a helpless, submissive little girl. Her father is looking forward to meeting Joel, who Maggie has said is her boyfriend.

Maurice and Joel are putting the dead body outside, where the sub-zero temperatures will preserve the body until they can decide what to do with it. Maggie and her father pass by, and Maggie quickly kisses Joel, who is thoroughly confused by her actions. Ho joins the two of them for lunch in the Brick, and Maggie convinces him, when her father isn't around, to play along with the charade. That night, over dinner, Joel not only discusses his hobby of bungee jumping, but also tells Frank O'Connell that he and Maggie have been discussing her conversion to Judaism. Frank accepts this with a nervous smile, and downs his drink.

After Shelly convinces Holling to have the circumcision, he has a dream where the operation is, to say the least, a failure. He wakes up bathed in sweat, and with Joel's help, is able to convince Shelly that the operation is unnecessary.

ANSWERS ON PAGE 149

TRIVIA TEASERS: TOWN OF CICELY

1) Who founded Cicely?

2) Where did Cicely and Roslyn move from?

3) What year was Cicely born?

4) What is the name for the area in which the town of Cicely resides?

5) Why is the "L" raised on Joel's office window?

6) Who painted the sign for Roslyn's Cafe?

7) Who painted the "'s" in the sign?

8) Why is the "'s" so small?

9) Who are the pilots in Cicely?

10) How many people live in Cicely?

11) What was the Brick's original name?

12) When did it first open?

13) What is the motto of the state of Alaska?

14) What is the radio frequency of KBHR?

15) When was the first Founders Day celebration?

Despite Joel's overzealous portrayal of Maggie's boyfriend, her father still likes him, and thinks they make a great couple. Maggie finally comes clean, and tells her father that her boyfriend is actually not Joel the doctor, but Rick the pilot. She tells him that she didn't want him to be disappointed in her, and Frank understands, and accepts her as she really is.

When no one arrives to claim the body of the unknown person, a funeral service is held, where Chris discusses life and death, and Maggie reads a Shakespearean sonnet, to which Shelly responds, "Boy, she sure can write!" After a few final words, Chris ignites the body, and it burns in a funeral pyre. Through the encounter with death, the characters learn to embrace life, and the show ends on a hopeful note.

"What I Did For Love"

Guest Starring: Elizabeth Huddle as Ingrid Klochner, Leo Geter as David Ginsberg

Co-Starring: Peg Phillips as Ruth-Anne

Featuring: Paul Fleming as Mr. Streisand, Pamela Abas-Ross as Woman #1, Dorothy Hanlin as Woman #2, Phil Lucas as Man, David A. Hrdlicka as Little Boy, Laura Kenny as Mrs. Streisand

Written by Ellen Kulman

Directed by Steven Robman

The episode fades in with Maggie and Joel playing Clue in what is obviously a dream sequence. However, Joel soon gets ready to leave, and puts on a black fedora. Maggie stops him, telling him to stay, and awakens in her own bed.

The next morning, Joel is in Ruth-Anne's store, buying souvenirs for his parents, who he is going to visit soon. Maggie comes in, and looks at Joel a little nervously. Joel, in an act of uncharacteristic kindness towards Maggie, offers to help her move her heavy chair into her cabin. At her cabin, Joel comments on the dioramas which she has built, as a memorial to each of her dead boyfriends. Each contains a miniature skeleton wearing a black fedora, which Maggie says symbolizes death. Her face shows that she recognizes one possible interpretation of her dream.

Chris In The Morning announces the annual Cicely Founders Day celebration, and mentions the rumors of lesbianism surrounding the town's two founders, Cicely and Roslyn. In the Brick, Maurice becomes upset, not wanting the town to be associated with homosexuality. However, his mood brightens when Ingrid walks in, a middle-aged lady who obviously knows Maurice well. We find that Ingrid is in town while her husband is off trapping, and that night, Maurice and Ingrid are in bed at Maurice's cabin. The two begin their activities, while a video of the moon rocket launch plays on the television in the background. These scenes with Maurice show a new side to his personality as a tenderness that has never before been apparent. For the first time, Maurice begins developing into a genuinely likable character, and Ingrid's love for him is evident in each of their scenes together.

Again, Maggie has a dream about playing Clue with Joel, but this time, they are joined by a third party as Mr. Streisand, who is dressed as death. He whispers to Maggie, "Let's not tell him about the Anchorage-New York plane crash." He then leans over to Joel, and shows him a picture of Miss Scarlet, who looks remarkably like Maggie. Again, Maggie awakens, now obviously disturbed by the dream.

At Maurice's cabin, in the middle of the night, Ingrid lies wide awake watching Maurice sleep. She is watching Maurice fearfully, and begins getting worried when his breathing stops, and then starts again after a long pause. This circumstance has obviously occurred before.

The next morning, we find Joel talking to Pete Gilliam about his temporary replacement, a doctor named David Ginsberg. Ingrid shows up to ask Joel about Maurice's spells of breathlessness. Joel is a bit surprised to hear of Maurice and Ingrid's activities, but agrees to talk to Maurice about the problem.

Maggie finds Chris, who is preparing his Founders Day ceremony, and seeks out his advice whether or not to tell Joel about her premonition. When Chris hears about the black fedora, he acts as if Joel is already dead. Knowing Maggie's past luck with men, and the significance of the dream, Chris believes that whatever Maggie does is fated. She finally decides to tell him and the agony over the decision shows her true concern for Joel.

Joel goes to visit Maurice, who refuses to let Joel watch him while he's asleep. Upon returning to his office, Joel is greeted by David Ginsberg, who is busy fixing the radiator. Although they are both from Flushing, the differences between the two are striking as David has boyish, blond-haired cuteness, and unlike Joel, is enamored with the idea of living in Cicely, if only for a short time. Because of their differences, Joel takes an immediate dislike to him, and even doubts his Jewish heritage. Ironically, David tells Joel that the in-flight movie from New York to Anchorage was *Marked For Death*. As Joel leaves the office, Maggie approaches him, and rather abruptly tells him of her dreams about the plane crash. Joel seems genuinely touched by her concern, but makes no plans to change his flight.

Later that night, Ed tries to convince Joel to sell his plane ticket, and Joel imagines what the town would be like if he died and was replaced by Ginsberg. The next day, at the Founders Day ceremony, Chris brings up Joel's impending death, and Maggie is shocked to find out that everyone in town knows about her dreams. Furthermore, they all believe that Joel is going to die, and they go around the room paying their respects. The whole interplay sickens Maggie, who storms out of the church.

After all the talk about death, Maurice finally consents to let Joel watch him sleep. As Joel drifts off to sleep in a chair by Maurice's bed, he dreams of being on a flight with Mrs. Streisand. Maggie is the flight attendant, who gives him a fedora before abandoning the plane. As Joel feels himself falling, he is awakened by Maurice. Joel informs him that he doesn't have a sleeping disorder, and Ingrid is relieved.

At Joel's office, Joel is sickened to find how easily David has integrated himself into the Cicelian community. This inherent dislike of Ginsberg, who has made himself at home in Joel's office, combined with the dream, convinces Joel to cancel his flight, and he hurriedly tosses David out into the cold.

That night, Maggie hears Joel out on her porch, and invites him in. He asks her why she is having dreams about him, trying to get her to admit her feelings towards him. Although she won't admit it, Joel agrees not to take the flight. After he leaves, Maggie puts on a tape and does a little dance. It is unclear whether her happiness is from relief, or from the knowledge of Joel's affection towards her.

"Spring Break"

Guest Starring: Diane Delano as Officer Barbara Semanski

Co-Starring: Peg Phillips as Ruth-Anne, John Mese as Gary McClellan, Jill Pierce as Knockout #1

Featuring: Mary Anderson as Knockout #2, Gregg Loughridge as Lumberjack, Gary Taylor as Logger

Written by David Assael

Directed by Rob Thompson

The show begins with Maggie and Joel walking through a lush, tropical jungle. While Maggie stares in wonderment, Joel complains about animals and tropical diseases. Maggie discovers a snake, and then pulls an apple off of a tree and offers a bite to Joel. After Joel takes a bite, Maggie points out that he's naked, and suddenly she is as well. Joel appears comfortable in his nakedness, and as Maggie begins kissing him, she awakens in bed with a groan.

Chris In The Morning establishes the premise for the episode, as he explains that the ice is preparing to crack. But until it does, the citizens of Cicely are affected in different ways. Joel enters Ruth-Anne's store looking for his lingerie catalog, and Ruth-Anne is glad to help his libido by giving him an issue of Playboy to read. Maggie enters shortly thereafter to return some videos, and both are a little nervous until Joel leaves. We find out that Maggie rented "Beefcake Bingo." When Joel returns to his truck, he finds that his radio has been stolen.

Joel visits Maurice, and complains about the theft. Maurice is quick to dismiss it, saying that the theft happens every spring, a result of temporary insanity. However, since there is usually no crime, there are no police to report to. Joel is unsatisfied, and leaves angry.

Back at the Brick, we find that Holling has undergone a personality change; instead of his normal, casual demeanor, Holling is adversarial, trying to pick a fight with everyone in the bar. Yet no one is willing to challenge him, even when he resorts to stomping on some toes.

The scene quickly cuts to Joel, who is in the middle of a Robert Palmer video, singing "Simply Irresistible" and surrounded by hordes of women. As the music cuts off, the women surround him, and tell him that they want him. Joel refuses at first, but is finally convinced to consummate his fantasy. This scene is one of the most entertaining of the show, and establishes a few of Joel's more interesting psychological traits. In fact, the entire episode is strengthened by the continual variety of interaction between the characters, and each of their various quirks.

The next day, Maurice's CD boombox is stolen, driving him to call the police. Officer Barbara Semanski arrives at his door, annoyed at having to drive in from Sourdough to investigate a stolen radio. Maurice is clearly attracted to her, both by her physical presence and her businesslike demeanor. After a little goading, Semanski ends up in Maurice's weight room and bench presses two hundred twenty pounds.

At Joel's office, he is preparing to dial a phone sex line, when Ed barges in and asks him several questions about the stolen radio. Ed has taken it upon himself to solve the mystery, but Joel is distracted by his overactive sex drive. Ed offers to pair Joel up with a girl he knows, but Joel politely refuses.

That night, the townspeople gather at the Brick for a potluck. Maggie runs into Joel in the kitchen, and they engage in a rather pointless argument covering everything from Jell-O to medical school. Right as the argument reaches its peak, Maggie and Joel freeze, their eyes locked. Their bodies smash together, and they begin kissing passionately, and somewhat clumsily, bouncing around the kitchen and knocking down pots and dishes. Just as quickly as they started, they stop, and as they pull back, Joel is shocked, and Maggie appears surprised and a little pleased. They rush out of the kitchen, trying to figure out what happened. Each person feels that they were the one who started it, and Joel and Maggie decide they both need to find a sexual partner, and run off in separate directions.

Later, Ed and Joel enter an igloo, and Ed introduces Joel to his cousin, who happens to look exactly like Maggie. Joel immediately warms to her, but she rejects him, and Joel wakes up in his office. That night at the Brick, Officer Semanski is asking around about the stolen radios, and Ed follows along with questions of his own. Hearing about her boxing prowess, Holling challenges Semanski to a fight, and she accepts. Later, in a moment of vulnerability, Maurice admits his deep affection for her, but she merely shrugs it off, and Maurice does not mention it again.

In Joel's office, Maggie comes in, speaking seductively and taking her top off as Joel stares. When she says something about catching a thief, Joel snaps out of his daydream, and finds that Ed is in the room with him. Ed claims he is zeroing in on the criminal.

That night, at the Brick, a boxing ring is set up for Barbara and Holling. Marilyn and Maggie are fervently knitting, presumably to relieve some of the sexual tension. Holling and Barbara exchange blows, but the cracking of the ice causes Holling to lose the desire to fight, and Barbara floors him. Maurice simply watches proudly.

Late that night, as Chris is finishing up his shift at KBHR, Ed comes in, having figured out that Chris is the thief. However, Ed does not know what action to take, so he simply asks Chris why he did it. The answer is, "Wildness, Ed, wildness!" Late that night, Joel arrives at Maggie's cabin in a panic. Although the ice has cracked, his desire for her hasn't lessened. He tells about his lustful thoughts, and Maggie shares her dreams, and they end their conversation in an orgasmic moment of mutual desire. After having cleared the air, the two share a cigarette.

The next morning, Joel arrives at the Brick for the annual Running of the Bulls, an all-male run through the streets of Cicely. As the race is about to start, Joel is shocked to find the men disrobing, and Holling informs him that the race is run in the buff. After a moment's thought, Joel smiles, accepts the madness, strips off his clothes, and runs through the streets of Cicely,

while the women of Cicely watch and cheer. In the final few moments, we sense Joel's final incorporation into the community.

ANSWERS ON PAGE 149

TRIVIA TEASERS: MAGGIE

1) What is Maggie's real name?

2) Where is Maggie from?

3) What is Maggie's father's name?

4) What record does Maggie's father hold?

5) What is Maggie's mother's name?

6) How old is Maggie's mother?

7) What is Maggie's profession?

8) What is the registry number of Maggie's plane?

9) When Joel first met Maggie, what did he think her profession was?

10) What title did Maggie hold when she was five?

11) What physical impairment does Maggie have?

12) What does Joel prescribe for her knee?

13) Who did Maggie come to Cicely with?

14) What was Dave's book titled?

15) What was the book about?

16) How did he die?

17) How did Bruce die?

18) How did Glenn die?

19) How did Harry die?

20) Who was Maggie's most recent boyfriend?

21) Had Rick ever been to college?

22) What was Rick's favorite tape?

23) How did he die?

24) Where does Maggie's brother live?

"War And Peace"

Guest Starring: Elya Baskin as Nikolai Ivanovich Apalanov, Dana Andersen as Lightfeather Duncan, Alan Fudge as Father Duncan

Co-Starring: Peg Phillips as Ruth-Anne, William James White Eagle as Dave the Cook

Written by Henry Bromell and Robin Green

Directed by Bill D'Elia

Holling is yelling at Dave the Cook, because he didn't get any sleep the night before, due to bad dreams. Shelly tells Holling to go see Dr. Fleischman. When he goes in, Holling asks Joel about his bad dreams, and Joel prescribes valium to help him sleep.

Back at the Brick, Nikolai shows up, a Russian gentleman who is familiar to everyone. He brings gifts for all his friends, and tells them that he decided to make his trip to Cicely early this year. Maurice enters, and tension fills the room. Maurice's hatred for Communism is obvious, and he is barely cordial to Nikolai. However, Nikolai is unfazed and sings a song.

At Ruth-Anne's store, Ed runs into a young woman named Lightfeather, and is immediately smitten. He later seeks out Chris for advice, and Chris tells him that he should write her a letter explaining how he feels. Ed agrees completely, but asks Chris to write the letter for him.

Joel stops by the Brick to check on Holling and meets Nikolai. He is very impressed, since he and Elaine saw Nikolai perform years ago in New York. However, Joel finds Holling in much worse condition. He is groggy and incoherent, and decides not to avoid his dreams anymore.

Several days later, Ed visits Whitefeather in her father's barn, and brings her a flower. Whitefeather says she was hoping for a letter, since she read the first one over and over again. Whitefeather is a very blunt, borderline obnoxious person, and is extremely turned on by the poem written by Ed. She begins kissing him, and pulls him down into the hay.

At the Brick, we find Maurice and Nikolai engaged in their annual chess match. Joel sits with a bored look on his face, while Maggie, Shelly, and the other townspeople watch raptly, and speak as if they were chess experts. After Maurice makes his move and hits the timer, Nikolai hits the timer and then moves his piece. Maurice is upset at this breach of regulations, and Nikolai accuses him of trying to weasel out of the game. Maurice finally challenges Nikolai to a duel.

Back at Whitefeather's barn, Ed and Whitefeather are laying in the hay, naked and covered in sweat. Ed has a smile pasted on his face, and they begin again as Ed reads more lines from the poem.

Everyone at the Brick is talking about the impending duel. After hearing about Holling's trouble with bad dreams, Nikolai tells him how Tolstoy got rid of his insomnia by working ceaselessly out in the fields for a whole day. He tells Holling to do something crazy and reckless in order to regain himself. The next night, Ed is having dinner at Whitefeather's house, while listening to Chris's radio reading of "War and Peace." Whitefeather's father seems to take a liking to Ed, but when Whitefeather hears Chris recite a line from Ed's poem, she realizes that he didn't really write it, and glares angrily at him.

Maggie and Joel are at a table in the Brick, discussing the upcoming duel. Maggie tries to explain the nobility and glamour of the whole event, while Joel sees it as simply barbaric. Shelly goes upstairs to find Holling, and she sees him packing his rifle and getting ready to head out into the wilderness.

Chris shows up at Ed's house, where Ed is lying on his bed watching Dr. Zhivago and crying. Chris apologizes for starting the chain of events, and Ed feels like he'll never get over the pain, but Chris knows that he will.

Outside in the snow it is morning and the duel commences. Maurice and Nikolai march nine paces, but before they can turn, Joel steps forward, breaks character, and says that the television audience would never accept such a duel. The other characters follow suit, complain about Joel stopping the scene, and then finally decide to go to the next scene. Although such a breaking of the fourth wall works on some shows, in this case it seems forced, and the show loses some of its magic.

Later that night, Maggie and Joel are at the Brick, and Maggie tells Joel how impressed she is that he took charge of the situation. Joel accepts her compliments, and believe that she is flirting with him. Holling shows up with a deer on a leash, and explains how he went out in the wilderness, fell asleep, and woke up with this deer next to him. His nightmares are gone, and the episode ends with Nikolai singing, and Maurice watching and smiling.

ANSWERS ON PAGE 149

"The Bumpy Road To Love"

TRIVIA TEASERS: MAURICE

1) How old is Maurice?

2) What was Maurice's profession?

3) Did he ever actually go into outer space?

4) What was the first thing Maurice did upon arriving in Cicely?

5) What was the second thing?

6) What was Maurice's brother's name?

7) Where is the Minnifield family crypt?

8) What is Maurice's nickname for the area around Cicely?

9) What did Maurice sing at Holling and Shelly's wedding?

10) What is Maurice's favorite musical?

11) According to Maurice, what were his fellow astronauts' favorite musicals?

12) What is Maurice's preferred after shave?

13) What is Maurice's birthmark?

14) What is Maurice's family name on the distaff side?

15) How old was Maurice when he entered the Marines?

16) How did he get in?

17) What title did Maurice's grandfather hold?

18) Where was his grandfather's farm located?

19) When was Maurice's house featured in House and Gardens?

20) Who gave Maurice the suit of armor in his house?

21) How did Maurice get his Cadillac?

Guest Starring: Valerie Mahaffey as Eve, Diane Delano as Officer Barbara Semanski, Catherine De Prume as Joanne, Adam Arkin as Adam

Co-Starring: Peg Phillips as Ruth-Anne, Grant Goodeve as Rick Pederson

Written by Martin Sage and Sybil Adelman

Directed by Nick Marck

As the new season starts, residents of Cicely are gathered near the woods at a ceremony for a statue of Rick which Maggie has commissioned. Maggie, however, thinks it looks like a hood ornament. As people are invited to say a few words about Rick, a young woman steps forward and introduces herself as Joanne. In a short testimony to Rick, she tells of their intimate relationship. Maggie is shocked. Later that afternoon, she and Maggie are talking at the Brick, and Maggie learns that Rick had several other relationships while she was living with him. Her sadness over Rick's death slowly turns to anger.

Maurice and Barbara Semanski are out in a field taking target practice with pistols. Barbara is aroused by the gunfire, and kisses Maurice passionately. Maurice chooses that moment to present her with a Browning which he had engraved to her. The thoughtfulness of the gift leaves her speechless. Barbara is obviously the female counterpart to Maurice as very gruff, bordering on masculine, with a tough, by-the-book demeanor that she devotes to her work as a police officer. At dinner that night, they dine with Holling and Shelly, and Maurice professes his love for Barbara, who is more concerned with her meal than with Maurice's affection.

Late that night, Joel is visited at his cabin by Adam, who tells him that his wife needs medical assistance. Joel is unwilling to go, but follows after Adam takes his medical bag. As the two take Joel's truck out to Adam's home, Adam speaks with unceasing praise about his wife, Eve. Despite Joel's cynicism, Adam proclaims his wife as the image of perfect womanhood. Upon arriving, Joel is confronted by a very outspoken woman, who is obviously an extreme hypochondriac. As Joel examines her, she is quick to point out her various symptoms, and makes her own diagnoses, which Joel refutes one by one. When Joel is unable to find anything wrong with her, she knocks him out with a frying pan to keep him from leaving.

Back in town, Maggie is drinking heavily at the Brick, and complains to anyone who will listen about how despicable men are. In a hilarious speech to Ed, Maggie concludes that men are only needed for sex, and are otherwise worthless. Ed, being a man, has absolutely no response for Maggie. Much later, Ruth-Anne shows up to take Maggie home. As Ruth-Anne is tucking Maggie in, Maggie asks why men are such swine. Ruth-Anne responds with a touching story about her deceased husband, and the affair that she had during the war. She tells Maggie that life is often confusing, but somehow we muddle through. She kisses Maggie tenderly on the forehead and leaves.

Joel awakens in Adam's cabin, only to find himself manacled hand and foot, with a large knot on his head. Eve explains her need for a 24-hour physician, and Joel refuses. However Eve, being a woman of great patience, tells Joel that she will wait. Eventually, after hours of starvation, she convinces Joel to eat, and Adam walks in as she is feeding him. The entire display disgusts Adam, who is obviously unaware that Joel is being held against his will. The two engage in a bitter argument, with Adam calling Eve a hypochondriac, and Eve calling Adam a pathological liar. Joel finally calls a halt to the argument, and demands that the two of them sit down so that they can discuss their differences.

As Maurice returns to his cabin in the evening, he is surprised to find Barbara preparing to leave. She tells him that she has returned his Browning, since she heard Maurice's accountant on the answering machine talking about tax loopholes for Maurice's return. Maurice is amused by the whole circumstance, and then his amusement turns to fear when he realizes that Barbara is seriously leaving him. She knows she can never respect him, after he broke the law. The door closes, and Maurice is left alone, speechless.

As Maggie lies asleep in bed, she dreams she is in heaven, which looks surprisingly like the Grosse Pointe Country Club. She is walking with Rick, who is there to answer some unresolved issues. Rick admits to sleeping with roughly 2500 women while he was with Maggie. He tells her that she needs someone steady to settle down with, like Joel. This is the last straw, and Maggie awakens from her dream.

In the woods, Joel is arbitrating the dispute between Adam and Eve. He eventually determines that the two of them should part ways, and never see each other again. However, his suggestion shocks them, and we see that they are meant for each other. Eve saws through Joel's chains, and the two of them walk Joel out to his truck. Joel chides them for not taking his advice, and Adam points out Joel's past luck with women, quoting Elaine's final letter to Joel, where she says, "Dear Joey. Take care. Don't get frostbite." This is one of many times where Adam seems omniscient, and Joel drives off in confusion.

Back at his office, Joel attempts to file through his manacles. In a strikingly honest moment, Maggie comes in and asks Joel if he would like to have dinner sometime. She almost leaves in embarrassment, but Joel accepts her offer, and she leaves with a smile on her face. The episode ends with Joel attempting to remove his manacles, and falling off the desk.

"Only You"

Guest Starring: Caitlin Clarke as Irene Rondenet

Co-Starring: Peg Phillips as Ruth-Anne, Heidi Swedberg as Linda, Denice Duff as Patti

Written by Ellen Herman

Directed by Bill D'Elia

As Joel and Chris walk down the streets of Cicely discussing food, every woman who walks by greets Chris, and many of them appear to be coming on to him. Joel finally stops Chris and asks what is going on, as a young woman comes up to Chris and kisses him. Joel is stunned. The two return to Joel's office, where Joel discovers an unusually high testosterone level. Chris explains that the uncontrollable attraction is a yearly occurrence, and has something to do with pheromones put out which only women can smell. Marilyn steps in to give Joel a message, but instead of leaving, stays a moment longer and stares at Chris with interest. Joel is fascinated by this unknown medical phenomenon.

In the middle of town, the Optomobile is visiting Cicely so everyone can get their eyes checked. Dr. Irene Rondenet examines Maggie, and tells her that she has presbyopia, which occurs as old age sets in. Maggie is disturbed by the news, since she is only twenty-nine. As she returns to the Brick, Joel explains that presbyopia is merely a harbinger of old age, and Maggie becomes even more worried. Meanwhile, Shelly gives Chris a burger on the house, Ruth-Anne invites him over for dinner, and he is escorted out by two women. Later he shows up at the Optomobile to have his eyes checked, and is surprised to discover that the female doctor is not at all affected by his smell.

The next morning, Joel drives up to Chris's trailer, where dozens of women are waiting, presumably to have their time with Chris. Joel tells Chris of his initial findings, and wants to run more tests. However, Chris is distracted, because he wants to go into town and see Dr. Rondenet. When he shows up at the Optomobile, she confirms his suspicion that she can't smell him, and is in fact not even attracted to him. Chris is more attracted by this fact, and begins obsessively thinking about Irene.

Back at his trailer, Chris emerges with Patty, and apologizes for his impotence. Lynn then emerges from the trailer, and he tells them that, although they were both fantastic, he is thinking about someone else. The women are amazed that anyone could resist him. Chris returns to town, where Joel is busily performing tests to try and determine the cause of this female attraction. The discussion of impotence piques Joel's interest, and Chris dotes on Irene, explaining that he is obsessed with her because she's not interested in him. He finally decides to muster up his courage, and heads over to the Optomobile. He proclaims his love for Irene, but she flatly refuses his advances.

The next day, Joel is surprised when he discover that women are no longer attracted to Chris. Chris realizes that it has gone away because he knows that Irene is leaving. He goes over to say goodbye in a very endearing speech. Irene is flattered by the attention, and begins closing up the Optomobile.

That evening, Maggie tells Joel of her fears that she is getting old. Joel responds by telling her that she has no problem with looks, that she is a knockout. If men aren't attracted to her, it's not because of her looks, but because of her abrasive personality. Maggie takes this as a compliment, ignorant of the insult Joel has paid her. As Chris prepares to sign off KBHR for the night, he looks out the window to see Irene driving away.

"Animals R Us"

Co-Starring: Peg Phillips as Ruth-Anne

Sparkle as Grandma Woody

Featuring: Harry Pringle as Crow Flies Straight, Bryson Liberty as Jerry the Indian, Kellee Bradley as Woman, Frank Welker as Special Dog Effects

Written by Robin Green

Directed by Nick Marck

In the morning of a typical day in Cicely, a small dog runs around town, catching glimpses of people in their daily activities. He passes by Ed, who enters Ruth-Anne's store to pick up his editing equipment. Maurice comes in to pick up some chicken soup, and is impressed by an ostrich egg by the cash register. Ruth-Anne comments that the egg came from one of Marilyn's ostriches. Maurice goes off to visit her, to discuss the business possibilities of raising ostriches.

While Maggie is gardening, the dog runs up to her and follows her as she goes inside. Obviously, Maggie has a weak spot for animals, and ends up letting it in. Maggie eventually brings the dog into Joel's office, so he can examine the dog for any parasites. Joel refuses, saying the examination would go against his ethics as a doctor. Besides, it is obvious that Joel is deathly afraid of the animal. The dog does not appear too fond of Joel either, and bites him, throwing Joel into a fit.

Ed is at the Brick, and has called Chris and Holling together to inform them that he's scrapping his movie project. Holling feels that his acting must not have been good enough, but Ed says that he knows when to cut his losses. He thanks them for their help, and leaves as Maggie and Joel enter with the dog. The dog jumps up on Rick's old stool at the end of the bar, and appears to want some of the beef jerky that is nearby. Holling makes an offhand comment that Rick was the only person who could stomach that beef jerky, and Maggie gets the start of an idea.

Later in the evening, she makes devil's mess eggs for the dog, who eats everything but the green peppers. Maggie remarks that Rick never liked green peppers either, and then becomes more suspicious when the dog stretches against the wall like Rick used to. The dog's link to Rick is obviously mostly Maggie's over-active imagination, but she tells the dog to bark three times if it is Rick, and it does.

Joel shows up at Ed's place, where Ed is forlornly playing the harmonica. Joel is obviously concerned about Ed's scrapping of his movie project, and as he talks with Ed, he looks through the screenplay. Ed defends his decision, since he's having an artistic crisis. After making comments about conversations with Corman, Scorese, Woody Allen, and Steven Spielberg, Ed tells an amazed Joel that he is pen pals with several big-name Hollywood directors. After the conversation ends, Ed feels renewed, and decides to continue work on his movie.

At Maurice's house, he is cooking dinner for Marilyn and trying to convince her to become partners with him in the ostrich business. Marilyn is wooed by the idea of easy money, and they toast a new partnership. In the Brick, Chris, Joel, Ed, and Shelly are talking, when Maggie enters and announces that the dog is actually Rick. Everyone seems to accept this concept, except for Joel, who refuses to entertain such an idea. The others chide him for not accepting the possibility of reincarnation, and Joel is once again bitten by the dog. Later, as Maggie is doing her gardening, she hears the dog speak with Rick's voice, and he expresses regrets about all of the other women he was involved with. Maggie is happy at this confession, and wakes up on her couch with the dog licking her face.

Maggie's mood is cheerful the next day, until she realizes that she's waiting on the dog hand and foot. She decides not to allow Rick to use her again, and kicks the dog out. However, when it returns with flowers in its mouth, Maggie forgives him. We see Maggie out on a picnic with the dog, drinking wine, playing frisbee, and basically having a great time. After an exciting day, Maggie shows up at the Brick, and Joel asks why she's all dressed up. Maggie explains to Joel that, although Rick is a dog, she's finally happy again. Joel is still cynical, and concerned about Maggie's mental and emotional state.

At Marilyn's ostrich farm, she informs Maurice that their partnership won't work, since his frequent visits have caused the ostriches to stop laying eggs. This leads Maurice to consider his abrasive personality, which he finally comes to terms with. Ed shows up in town to invite everyone to the opening of his movie which pleases Joel.

A visitor shows up at Maggie's place to pick up her dog. Maggie is obviously upset and sad to find out that the dog is actually just a mooch. When she returns to town and runs into Joel, she tells him that maybe she did need to work out some things, and maybe she did work them out with a dog, but the dog was Rick. Joel, foregoing the opportunity to make a cutting remark, is merely quiet and sympathetic.

As Ed's movie begins, the viewer is treated to glimpses of life around Cicely. Dr. Fleischman's office, Ruth-Anne's store, and Maurice's home are all pictured. Ed's narration tells that sometimes people leave Cicely, and the shot is of Maggie and the dog going out on a picnic. Joel looks over at Maggie with concern, and finds that she has tears in her eyes. In this one moment, they are both vulnerable, and it seems that things may work between them after all. As the movie ends, Ed smiles, satisfied with his work.

"Jules et Joel"

Guest Starring: Diane Delano as Officer Barbara Semanski, Douglas Rowe as Buddy

Co-Starring: Peg Phillips as Ruth-Anne, John Procaccino as Jerry

Featuring: Lou Hetler as Sigmund Freud, Gary Taylor as Man In Street, Shelley Henning as Woman In Cab, Dave Guppy as Logger, Ben DiGregorio as Cab Driver, Robert J. Zenk as Patient

Written by Stuart Stevens

Directed by James Hayman

On Halloween night, Joel is visited by a man in a devil suit who demands candy. Since Joel has none, and is unwilling to give up his TV dinner, the man sprays Joel with silly string. Joel chases after him, hitting his head on a wooden support and knocking himself unconscious.

The next day, a cab pulls into town, and out comes a slick gentleman who looks remarkably similar to Joel. After kissing the girl in the backseat goodbye, and paying the cab fare, the driver heads back to New York. Maggie spots the man on the street, and thinks it's Joel. The gentleman is very open in responding to Maggie's attention. However, when Maggie enters the Brick, she is surprised to find Joel eating. She thinks Joel is playing a trick on her, and Joel is confused by her reaction.

Once she describes the man outside, Joel exclaims, "Oh no!" and runs to his office, where he is greeted by Jules, his twin brother. Jules explains that he needed to get away from New York for a while, and will be staying in Cicely. Later at the Brick, Jules plays slight-of-hand tricks on Maurice and Ed, and is obviously a con man. Joel escorts him outside, where they run into Maggie. Maggie is surprised at the similarity, and seems impressed by Jules, who is more likable than Joel. Jules and Joel agree to switch places for a day, like they did when they were children, in order to give each of them a break from their normal lives for a little while.

In Joel's office, Joel is dressed as Jules, and is practicing his strong New York accent. However, Marilyn and Ed are not taken in by the switch, since Indians are not fooled by appearances. Maggie, though, does not see the switch, and so Joel has an opportunity to ask Maggie about her feelings for him, through the personality of Jules.

At KBHR, Chris receives a call from Frank Watson, otherwise known as the Mad Bomber. Frank used to be in jail with Chris's father, and Frank now wants Chris to help him turn himself in. Chris is very uncomfortable talking to Frank, and knows how dangerous the man can be. At Chris's hesitation to help, Frank becomes more angry, and says he will call again later. Chrisis visibly shaken.

That night, Joel is at the Brick playing Jules, and dealing a game of three-card monte. Officer Semanski, who is in the neighborhood visiting Maurice, arrests Joel and drags him off to jail. In his cell, Joel sheds the Jules persona, and demands a call. His cellmate is an elderly gentleman with an accent, who acts like a psychiatrist. Eventually, Joel discovers that the man claims to be Sigmund Freud, and Joel goes along with him long enough to be psychoanalyzed.

Joel explains how, as a child, he used Jules as a scapegoat when he did something bad. He felt that a blemish wouldn't hurt Jules' already soiled reputation. Freud latches on to the word "soiled," and attempts to draw Joel's potty-training experiences out of him. Joel admits an affection for Jules' openness; Joel feels the need to always be in control of himself, and is thus cold towards Maggie, when he actually wants to lick her naked body from head to foot

ous, and asks Freud' opinion, but finds him fast asleep.

Chris is waiting in the woods for Frank, who has agreed to give himself up to the authorities. When he arrives, he is wired with dynamite, which does little to relax Chris. Frank is obviously very sensitive about his height, and Chris has to talk fast to keep Frank from detonating himself. They finally leave the forest together.

At Maggie's place, Jules is dressed as Joel, and having dinner with Maggie. Although dressed as Joel, Jules is still very forward, and Maggie is somewhat attracted to 'Joel' and his newfound spontaneity. Jules eventually ends up hitting on Maggie, and is practically on top of her on the couch, when the phone rings, and it is Joel, waiting to be let out of jail. After picking him up, Jules reassures Joel that he could never get anywhere with Maggie, that she's more attracted to Joel's type of person.

After Jules leaves the next day, Joel is having dinner with Maggie, and trying to be more spontaneous. As we see them both smiling and enjoying themselves, the camera pulls back, and we fade into Joel laying in bed with a bandaged head. Maggie and Ed are in Joel's cabin, taking care of Joel, who hit is head at the beginning of the episode and is just now regaining consciousness. After telling them about his dream, Joel remembers that he doesn't have a twin brother. Joel remembers some of the people from his dream, in an ending very reminiscent of The Wizard Of Oz, and Maggie

ANSWERS ON PAGE 149

TRIVIA TEASERS: HOLLING

1) Where was Holling born?

2) When was Holling born?

3) What is Holling's middle name?

4) How old was Holling's father when he died?

5) How old was Holling's mother when she died?

6) How old was Holling's grandfather when he died?

7) How old was Holling's grandmother when she died?

8) What is Holling's cousin's name?

9) What is Holling's uncle's name?

10) How old was Charlie when he died?

11) What was Holling's original family name?

12) What was Holling' great-great-grandfather's name?

13) How big was Jesse the bear?

14) How did Jesse lose his toe?

15) When did Holling stop killing for sport?

16) When did Jesse come into Cicely for the first time?

17) How many stitches did Holling get when Jesse clawed him?

18) Who got a pin in his jaw because of Holling?

from his dream, in an ending very reminiscent of The Wizard Of Oz, and Maggie and Ed leave Joel alone to rest, as "Somewhere Over The Rainbow" plays in the background.

"The Body In Question"

Guest Starring: Allan Miller as Elijah

Co-Starring: Peg Phillips as Ruth-Anne

Featuring: William J. White as Dave the Cook, Sharon Collar as Woman, Shmuly Levitin as Yo'el, Gabriel Salvador as Tellakutan

Written by Henry Bromell

Directed by David Carson

While fishing out in a river, Chris is surprised to find a boot floating among the ice from the spring thaw. It is followed by a French flag floating along the river, and when he looks upriver, Chris spots a figure frozen in a block of ice. The body is taken to the Brick, where it is examined by Maurice, Joel, and several townspeople. Holling, who has French heritage, begins translating a diary found near the body, and discovers that the man is Pierre

LaMoulin, and the diary is dated April 2, 1814. To Joel's wonderment, everyone seems to believe this dairy, which also indicates that Napoleon was not actually at Waterloo, changing the face of history books to come.

At his office, Joel examines a tissue sample from the body, and determines that it is in fact human. Maurice is pleased by this finding, and encourages Joel to perform more tests to determine the age of the body. Joel reluctantly agrees, and returns to the Brick to take more samples. There, he runs into Maggie, who is reading further into the diary. She is engrossed in the soap-opera story of Pierre, and Joel is bothered by the apparent conflict between the diary and historical records. Maggie simply accepts the idea that history may have been wrong.

That night, Holling appears to be preoccupied with something, and Shelly is surprised to find that he doesn't want to fool around. After having heard of the relationship between Napoleon and Elba, Shelly believes that Holling no longer wants to be with her, and begins doubting her own self. She goes to see Joel, and cites her previous hysterical pregnancies as evidence that she is barren. Her concern is over the idea that, if Holling finds out, he may choose to dump her for someone who can give him a son. Joel sees no connection between the events, and tells Shelly that she has put two and two together and gotten twenty-two. Nevertheless, Shelly is still concerned.

While Joel is busy testing the fabric to determine its age, Marilyn tells him of the Tellakutan tribe, who are believed to be of French descent. She says that this legend coincides with the diary, which says that Napoleon landed in Alaska, and preceded to marry a native woman named Moshka. Joel begins to think that the concept of Napoleon arriving in Alaska instead of Waterloo might actually have some basis in fact.

At Shelly's behest, Joel visits Holling at the Brick, and asks him why he no longer wants to fool around. He tells Joel that the arrival of Pierre has reminded him if his own tainted bloodline. According to Holling, his entire family line is pure evil, descendants of French bluebloods. Since Holling is the last Vincoeur alive, he wants to end the line, and avoid a "genetic Chernobyl."

The evening finds Joel sitting alone outside the Brick, thinking. Maggie asks him what is wrong, and Joel says that he is depressed because he's starting to believe in Pierre. The actuality of his existence has thrown Joel's finely-honed scientific and historical beliefs out the window, and Joel can no longer be sure of anything. Maggie, who easily accepts Pierre, can not understand his dilemma.

A town meeting is held by Maurice to determine what will be done with Pierre. Maurice's plan is to make Pierre's frozen body the main attraction in a Cicely Historical Museum, complete with underground parking garage and adjoining mall. Chris, however, urges him to consider the metaphysical implications of changing history by revealing Pierre's past. He feels that the discovery the Napoleon was not at Waterloo could have far-reaching effects on the entire universe. In an entertaining verbal interplay, Joel stands up to debate Chris, saying that the world has an obligation to know the truth. The whole concept of facts versus truth is bantered about for a while, and is interrupted by the entrance of three Indians wearing sunglasses, who announce in French that they have come for the body.

Late at night, Joel is in the freezer at the Brick, looking at the body of Pierre and considering his own heritage. He falls asleep, and dreams that he is talking with Elijah, while watching his great-grandfather perform the Passover ceremony. Elijah chides

Joel for never actually believing in him, and Joel considers the place of Elijah in his own philosophy. When he awakens, blue and shivering, he runs off the Maurice's house, and tells Maurice that he believes that the Tellakutans have been waiting for Pierre just as the Jews have been waiting for Elijah. Considering Pierre's place in their belief system, it would be wrong to keep the body.

After much debate, Holling decides to tell Shelly of his tainted heritage, and she says the she doesn't care about his ancestry, and she knows that he is a good person. This satisfies Holling, who goes downstairs to check on the body. He opens the door to find the freezer defrosted, with only Pierre's hat lying in a pool of water. On the radio, Chris later announces Pierre's disappearance, and the Tellakutans are seen in a canoe, paddling Pierre's body off into the mist as Marilyn stands watching.

"Roots"

Guest Starring: Jessica Lundy as Elaine Schulman, Richard Cummings Jr. as Bernard, Adam Arkin as Adam

Co-Starring: Peg Phillips as Ruth-Anne, African Dance Sequences by Djimbe West African Drummers and Dancers, and Ceedo Senegalese Dance Company

Written by Dennis Koenig

Directed by Sandy Smolan

In the middle of the night, Chris wakes up to the sound of African music outside his trailer. He peers out and sees hundreds of drummers and dancers in native African garb dancing in a circle. After watching for a minute, Chris begins to feel the rhythm, and dances along with them. Suddenly, they disappear, and Chris is left dancing alone in the middle of a field.

As Joel takes his morning shower, he screams as pieces of plaster from his roof fall on him. He jumps out of the shower, and is greeted by Maggie, who is working on his roof. Joel complains about the hole in his roof, and decides to run into town. Along the way, he is passed by a car carrying Chris's half-brother Bernard, who has returned to see Chris at KBHR. The two of them greet each other warmly, and their strange mental connection is apparent as they simultaneously go off to the Brick. Bernard has come to Cicely to bring Chris 36,000 dollars, which is one half of their father's inheritance, plus interest. Chris refuses the money, saying that his father, who was spiritually a different man from Bernard, would never have left him any money. Bernard is confused, but accepts Chris's decision.

In Joel's office, Adam walks in and demands that Joel lend him a hundred dollars to pay his insurance premium. Joel refuses, and their argument is interrupted by Marilyn's announcement that Elaine, Joel's ex-fiancee, has arrived. Joel is speechless as Elaine enters, and informs him that Dwight, who she left Joel for, has suddenly died. Joel kicks Adam out of the office, and Elaine and Joel are obviously both uncomfortable with the reunion. Elaine tells Joel that she wanted to see him, but was afraid to call, because he might have told her not to come. Joel says that he definitely would have told her not to, and says that it was a mistake for her to come. Elaine leaves in tears, and Joel sits down in disbelief.

Joel and Adam are having lunch at the Brick, and Joel is pouring his heart out to Adam about Elaine. Adam appears more concerned about how terrible the food is. Criticism of the food causes Holling to challenge him to do better, a wager which Adam can't refuse. As Adam retires to the kitchen, Maggie runs in to tell Joel that Elaine is in her truck sobbing. Joel obviously does not care, and is angry and bitter at Elaine. Maggie sees his behavior as self-centered, and convinces him that Elaine is reaching out for a friend to talk to. Joel relents, and the three of them ride up to Joel's cabin together. Things are still very uncomfortable between Elaine and Joel, but Maggie does her best to keep Joel acting civil.

At his cabin, Joel finds Elaine crying in the bathroom because she forgot her toothbrush. He offers to let her use his toothbrush, but Elaine refuses, knowing that Joel doesn't really want her to. As Joel lays on the couch, he talks to Elaine, who is laying in Joel's bed. Elaine apologizes for their whole breakup, and says that part of her wishes she had never met Dwight. Joel is still bitter, and does not accept her apology.

That night, Chris and Joel are cooking hot dogs over a campfire outside Chris's trailer, and Chris asks Bernard about his dreams. While Chris's dreams have been vivid and colorful, Bernard's have been rather bland and mundane. This difference between them piques Chris's curiosity, and he ponders Bernard's situation. As they fall asleep, Chris's dream of African dancers now includes Bernard, who merely stands by watching. Chris and Bernard stand watching the dancers, and speaking casually in Swahili. When Chris awakens, he realizes that he must go to Africa.

The next morning, Joel awakens to find Elaine standing shivering by his bed. The bedroom is freezing because of the whole in the roof, and Joel invites Elaine in his bed so she can keep warm. Lying back to back, the two of them reminisce about their past relationship, and Maggie bursts in to find the two of them lying in bed together and laughing. She is suddenly uncomfortable, and quickly leaves. Later, she talks with Shelly at the Brick, where everyone is thrilled by Adam's culinary expertise. Maggie's jealousy is obvious, and she tries to explain away the fact that Joel and Elaine were in bed together. However, Shelly is unable to offer any reasonable explanation.

On KBHR, Chris declares himself to be a person of color, and he announces to Cicely his intent to travel to Africa, using the money provided by Bernard. Meanwhile, Maggie enters Joel's office with a hurt wrist, obviously a sympathy ploy to get attention from Joel. Joel, however, is uncaring, and merely asks how the injury will affect his roof work. Maggie is enraged, and Joel misses her innuendos that he and Elaine slept together. Maggie's departure leaves Joel in confusion.

That night, Elaine and Joel are having dinner at the Brick, and they are joined by Maggie, who is obviously out of place. She tries to convince Elaine to join her at the dump to watch the bears, but Joel and Elaine say they are tired, and Maggie uneasily watches them leave. Returning to Joel's place, Elaine finds her second wind, and they begin kissing passionately, and drop to the floor.

Chris's dream again contains the tribal dancers, but they are joined by a king, who turns out to be Bernard in a mask. Bernard tells him that Chris has been having his dreams, and the two wake up simultaneously. Chris hypothesizes that somehow, the two of them got their wires crossed, and so Bernard is actually the one who needs to go to Africa.

The next morning, Maggie is sitting at the bar in the Brick, and Adam serves her a virgin mary and tells her to go home. Playing the bartender role, Adam begins psychoanalyzing Joel, using information which he cannot possibly know about Joel. Maggie argues his analysis, and Adam turns to analyzing her instead. Not only does he know her full name, but he also knows personal facts about her childhood and her father, to Maggie's confusion. He concludes that Maggie will end up old, alone, with lots and lots of cats. This entire scene is wonderful, and pairs up two characters who heretofore have had little interaction. Their personality conflict puts Maggie's entire range of personal problems into sharp focus, and makes her realize her feelings for Joel.

At Joel's place, Elaine and Joel talk about how great the sex was, and Joel realizes that they finally have closure to their relationship. At the same time, they both know instinctively that the relationship is over, and Elaine appears regretful.

At his office, Maggie finds Joel staring out the window, deep in thought. Maggie tries to convince Joel that Elaine is after his money, but Joel responds by telling her that Elaine is gone. In a rare moment of total honesty between them, Maggie asks Joel if he's okay, to which Joel replies, "I'm fine...thanks for asking." He smiles warmly, and the two of them leave the office, and walk down the street together.

"A-Hunting We Will Go"

Guest Starring: Peg Phillips as Ruth-Anne

Written by Craig Volk

Directed by Bill D'Elia

In the early afternoon, Chris In The Morning is reminiscing about his hunting exploits as a child, as people around town are in the midst of hunting season. Maggie drives into town with a ten-point buck tied to her car, and Joel argues with her, obviously bothered by the hunting frenzy. Returning to his office, he examines Ruth-Anne, who is currently mending a broken foot. She tells Joel that Ed is helping her with work around the store so that she can allow her foot to heal.

As Joel leaves work that afternoon, he runs into Chris and Holling, who are making preparations for tomorrow's hunting trip. Holling is reluctant to be gone for more than one day, since he would rather be with Shelly. With honest curiosity, Joel asks what the attraction is to hunting. Chris explains that humans are by nature predators, and Joel asks to come along on the hunting trip. Chris and Holling reluctantly agree.

The next morning, Joel is in Ruth-Anne's store buying supplies for the trip. When Maggie hears that he intends to go hunting, she is surprised, and a little pleased. However, she obviously believes that he will still hate it when he returns. While helping out at the store, Ed discovers that it is Ruth-Anne's birthday when she receives a card from her son Matt. Upon finding out that Ruth-Anne is seventy-five, Ed starts to see her as near death, and becomes over-protective. He barely allows Ruth-Anne to walk around by herself, and treats her as if she were made of glass. Needless to say, Ruth-Anne is not thrilled by his coddling, and tells him to stop it.

Joel shows up to meet Chris and Holling in a bright orange vest and hat, and Chris and Holling are amused by Joel's lack of hunting expertise. Joel is getting psyched for the trip, and asks to see his shotgun. They leave, as Maurice acts as DJ, and talks about the joy of hunting. When they arrive in the forest, Joel learns how to lock and load his shotgun, and is exhilarated by the feeling of firing it. Chris advises him to wait, so that he can shoot at a moving target.

Holling flushes some grouse out, and Joel fires, but misses, while Chris gets two. Holling wants to return home right away to see Shelly, but Joel is unhappy that he missed, and wants to try again. Holling reluctantly agrees to stay another day, and they set up camp for the night.

At Ruth-Anne's store, Ed expresses his concern for Ruth-Anne's meat intake, and is disgusted when she lights up a cigarette. Maurice enters to buy some supplies, but his conversation about death with Ed only makes matters worse, and Ed is more worried than before.

At two in the morning, Joel wakes up and tries to get Holling and Chris up for a day of hunting. Chris tells Joel that it is too early, and advises him to get some sleep. However, Joel lies awake, and comments about the primal roots of hunting, and howls at the moon. The next morning, after a word of advice from Chris, Joel tries again, and wings a grouse. But when he finds it fluttering on the ground, he is unable to wring its neck and finish it off. The scene changes to Joel's office, where he, Chris, and Holling rush in with the bird on a stretcher. Joel frantically prepares for surgery.

At the Brick that night, Chris and Holling talk about Joel's psychic wound incurred from the gunshot blast. Maggie overhears their conversation, and is amazed to discover that Joel actually hit something. She visits him at his office, where he is vigilantly keeping watch over the injured bird. She tells him that a grouse's life is short, and he should let it die. When it eventually passes on, Joel's sadness turns to depression, and he ends up at home watching movies like *Old Yeller* and *White Fang*. Maggie visits him, and is for once sympathetic of his depression. Joel, in turn, admits to her that she was right about the joy of hunting; the killing was great, but he couldn't take the dying.

The next night, Ruth-Anne's car won't start and Chris escorts her over to the Brick to get a jumpstart. When she enters, she finds a surprise party that Ed has organized, and receives presents from everyone. Joel is finally up and about again, and eats a bite of grouse, which he admits is actually good. He seems to have come to terms with the death of his bird. As Ruth-Anne finishes opening her presents, Ed gives her a jar of dirt, which is part of her present. The next day, the two visit a spot at the edge of a cliff, overlooking a beautiful forest tableau. Ed explains that he bought the plot of land for Ruth-Anne's grave. Ruth-Anne is at first shocked by the reminder of her death, but then thanks Ed for picking such a beautiful spot, and allowing her a chance to dance on her own grave. As the camera pulls back, Ruth-Anne and Ed begin dancing happily on the plot of dirt.

ANSWERS ON PAGE 149

TRIVIA TEASERS: SHELLY

1) Where is Shelly from?

2) Who was Shelly married to in high school?

3) How old is Wayne?

4) What title did Shelly win before arriving in Cicely?

5) Who was a judge at that contest?

6) What is Shelly's father's name?

7) What is Shelly's mother's name?

8) How many times was Shelly's father married?

9) What song was played before Shelly and Holling's wedding?

10) What is Shelly's aunt's name?

11) Who always kisses Shelly on the cheek?

12) What was the name of Shelly's pet angel fish?

13) Who is Shelly's best friend from high school?

14) Where did Cindy graduate from college?

15) What were her major and minor?

"Get Real"

Guest Starring: Richard Brestoff as Steve, Judith Kahan as Adrienne, Remy Ryan as Nina, Bill Irwin as Enrico Bellati, the Flying Man

Co-Starring: Peg Phillips asRuth-Anne

Featuring: Armenia Miles as Mrs. Whirlwind, Reginald Ward as Mr. Whirlwind, Dan Perkins as Handsome Man and Cirque du Soleil as the Ludwig Bichtenstein Masquerade and Reality Company

Written by Diane Frolov and Andrew Schneider

Directed by Michael Katleman

On a small backwoods road, Ed is fixing a flat tire when he spots a crowd of people trudging towards him. The group is apparently a circus troupe whose tour bus has broken down. Ed points them towards Cicely, only a half mile away. He watches them pass in awe and wonder.

On KBHR, Chris announces that the Ludwig Bichtenstein Masquerade and Reality Company has made an unscheduled stop in Cicely, thanks to a broken-down school bus. The troupe is seen in the middle of town, gathered around their towed bus. Jugglers, children, and a bear mill around, and a young girl asks her father Steve, who heads the troupe, for her allowance. A man separates himself from the group, and begins silently following Marilyn. Through note cards, he tells her that he is the Flying Man, and is interested in her. Marilyn replies that she's available, but not interested, and the Flying Man is left alone as she walks off.

At the Brick, Steve is entertaining Chris with magic, using the Heisenberg Uncertainty Principle as a possible explanation for his mystical abilities. He and Chris then embark on a discussion of physics and the nature of reality. Steve, who received his Ph.D. in Physics at Berkeley, is amazed at Chris's knowledge, which comes solely from personal reading.

At Joel's office, Ed helps him look through his medical books, and Joel expresses his desire to study for the Board Medical Examination to gain an additional specialty. Since he will have to study night and day, he tells Ed that he won't be out very much, and Ed understands. In the waiting room, Joel finds Enrico Bellati waiting for Marilyn with flowers and a vase. Marilyn still refuses to go out with him, but after he refuses to leave, she finally gives in.

Joel is walking down the street reading, but finds himself occasionally distracted by the bustle of the circus going on around him. Adrienne, Steve's wife, passes by Joel on her way to Ruth-Anne's store to buy some disks for her daughter's laptop. As Maggie watches, Adrienne reads Ruth-Anne's palm, and very accurately describes past events of her life, as well as the fact that she will fall in love again. Maggie is impressed by the accuracy of the reading, as well as its hopeful nature.

As Ed is quizzing Joel in his office, Marilyn announces that she is leaving for her date. She and Enrico Bellati end up having dinner with Marilyn's parents, who say close to nothing. Enrico, who does not speak at all, merely responds with polite nods and appreciative hand gestures. Mrs. Whirlwind leans over to Marilyn, and tells her that she likes Enrico, to which Marilyn smiles.

The next day, Marilyn and the Flying Man are having a picnic by a pond, and feeding the ducks. The two have grown close, and Enrico asks her to marry him. Marilyn understands his complex hand gestures flawlessly, and tells him that she'll consider his offer.

Much later, Joel is driving into town while trying to memorize part of his medical book. On his way in, he passes the Flying Man, who refuses the ride because he is going to fly into town. Joel laughs and drives off, and as he pulls into town, he passes the Flying Man again, who is now sweaty and visibly exhausted. Ed meets Joel, and asks what they're going to work on, but Joel is amused by the circus preparations going on around him, and decides to take a break.

At the Brick, Maggie nervously approaches Adrienne to have her palm read. Adrienne sees many aspects of Maggie's personality, and detects a long lifeline. When Maggie asks specifically about love, Adrienne tells her, rather nervously, that she will have a tall, muscular, outdoorsy husband, and three lovely girls. However, the tone of her voice leads Maggie to conclude that she won't be happy.

At Marilyn's house, Enrico Bellati shows up, and Marilyn tells him that she can't go with him. He is saddened, and know that he can't stay in Cicely. Marilyn watches with regret as he departs.

After Maggie leaves the Brick, she passes by Joel, who is trying to juggle, and wants her to watch. She dismisses him, and spots a handsome man with long blond hair smiling at her. She looks back at Joel, who is clumsily juggling, and then approaches the man. Although he is her perfect man, and she knows that the sex would be great, she tells him that it's just not enough, and goes back to watch Joel juggle.

"Seoul Mates"

Guest Starring: Kim Kim: Yung Yong Ja, Kwi Hyun Song: Yung Duk Won, Chi-Muoi Lo: Yung Bong Joo

Co-Starring: Peg Phillips: Ruth-Anne, William J. White: Dave the Cook

Written by: Diane Frolov and Andrew Schneider

Directed by: Jack Bender

On KBHR, Chris In The Morning announces preparations for the annual Raven Pageant, a holiday tradition in Cicely. Maurice is depressed because he is alone during the holidays and stops by to talk to Chris. Just then Shelly enters and tells Maurice that there are people to see him. Two Korean men and one woman are waiting to talk to him. The younger man introduces himself as Bong Joo, the other man as Duk Won, and the woman as Yong Ja. Maurice is confused, and asks why they are there to see him. Bong says that Duk Won is Maurice's son.

Joel watches eagerly as Ed and Dave unload a Christmas tree for the Brick, and talks about how much he's always liked Christmas trees. When Ed asks if Joel would like to have one, Joel reminds Ed that he is Jewish. However, despite his heritage, Joel has always loved Christmas. Maggie enters and trips over a pile of logs. Joel tells Maggie that this is a subconscious indication that she doesn't want to go home for Christmas.

Maurice enters the Brick to find his son, along with Duk Won's mother and son, sitting at a table. He tells them that Bong Ja's story checks out, and that he may have committed some improprieties in Korea when he was sixteen. However, Bong is apparently the only one who understands any English, so he has to translate for the others. Maurice asks them how much money they want, and Bong tells him that Duk wanted to meet his father. Despite this show of affection, Maurice's paranoia causes him to fear a lawsuit.

At Joel's cabin, Ed and Bong carry in a Christmas tree. Joel goes on for a while comparing Christmas and Hanukkah. When Ed is about to leave, Joel asks what he should do with the tree. He later talks to the tree, saying that his ownership of the tree does not betray his own religious beliefs. Maggie stumbles in to see him with a hurt ankle and comments on the tree. Joel gets defensive becuase he is Jewish and owns a tree. Maggie is more concerned with her impending trip home, and knows that she will soon find a round-trip ticket to Grosse Pointe in the mail.

Back at Maurice's cabin, the Yung family has apparently moved in for a few days. As Maurice brings in the laundry, he apologizes to Yong Ja for his corduroys bleeding in the wash, ruining her kimono. He offers to buy a new one, but she refuses. Maurice appears genuinely sad and regretful when he tells her that, although he's been trying, he can't seem to remember her. Although she can't understand what he's saying, the sentiment is clear. After expressing his regrets, Maurice rather bluntly comments that she would probably be more happy with someone of her own "persuasion." This comment is based on Maurice's egocentric belief that she returned to marry him. When he makes that comment, Yong is obviously hurt and sad.

At Ruth-Anne's store, Joel comes in to buy Christmas tree ornaments, but all Ruth-Anne carries are raven lights and raven ornaments. Maggie shows up to pick up her mail, and finds the expected letter from home. Upon opening it, she finds that her parents have decided to go to St. Thomas this year by themselves. Joel tells Maggie that now she can relax, and Maggie agrees, but she is obviously bothered by the fact that her parents didn't even invite her to visit. She plays off her disappointment and quickly leaves.

The Minnifield household is having dinner, and in the middle, Duk calls Maurice "Dad." Clearly, Maurice feels uncomfortable with this show of affection, especially from a grown man. Duk begins pouring his heart out to Maurice, but Maurice is unfeeling and unresponsive. Finally, Bong puts on a tape, and Duk sings "Fly Me To The Moon" to Maurice, making him even more uncomfortable.

Later that night, Maurice is walking around town by himself and runs into Chris, who breaks off from the carolers to talk to Maurice. Maurice is bothered by his family, disappointed that his son is "a middle-aged Chinaman," and generally annoyed by the fact that Duk's not white. However, he also feels guilty for rejecting his own flesh and blood. Chris simply tells Maurice that it's learned behavior, and it can be unlearned. He walks off, leaving Maurice alone with his conscience.

The next day, at Maurice's, he tells Duk that he'd love to take a hike with him, but he has some work to do in his office. He rather sheepishly returns to his office, trying to avoid facing up to his prejudice. Yong bursts in on Maurice, with Bong by her side translating. She tells Maurice that her son wanted to see his father for Christmas, and when Maurice tries to interrupt, she cuts him off. Maurice is quiet as she tells him that it was mistake, that they never should have come. She is on the verge of tears as she leaves. Maurice finally hears her words, and invited Duk to have dinner with him at the Brick.

Over dinner, he tells Duk that, although he's not the son Maurice bargained for, Maurice is still his father. Duk is without a translator, so he has trouble understanding, but they soon begin communicating. When Maurice asks him what he does for a living, expecting Duk to be a barber or a tailor, he is amazed to find that his son is an electrical engineer. He even shouts out proudly, "Hey guys, he's an engineer." For the first time, a sense of respect comes into Maurice's eyes. He pats him on the shoulder, and notices that Duk is rather muscular. Duk looks Maurice straight in the eye, slides the glasses aside, and puts his elbow down on the table, in a challenge position. A look of determination crosses Maurice's face, and they arm wrestle, with Maurice beating Duk only after a tough battle. But after the match, Maurice has gained more respect for his son.

Maggie arrives at Joel's cabin to help him decorate his tree on Christmas Eve. After giving him a few simple pointers about how to put ornaments on, she says she's going to leave and work on her taxes. Joel is shocked, and reminds her that it's Christmas Eve, but Maggie tells him that she's not in the mood, and leaves. Hours later, Joel shows up at Maggie's cabin, where she is alone with her taxes. He tells her to close her eyes, walks her outside, and when she opens them, she sees a magnificently lit and decorated tree. Joel explains that under it all he is still a Jew, and the tree belongs to her. He wishes her a merry Christmas, and her spirit is restored.

As Maurice returns home that night, Yong is performing a Christmas prayer. He tells her with great honesty and sincerity, that she should be proud of the son she raised. He tells her that Duk is a strong man, and Yong says "big and strong" in Korean. Suddenly, Maurice's face lights up, as he remembers that "big and strong" was her nickname for him back in Korea. Suddenly it all comes back to him. He looks at her and asks quietly, "So how are you?"

"Dateline: Cicely"

Guest Starring: Adam Arkin: Adam

Co-Starring: Peg Phillips: Ruth-Anne

Featuring: Gary Taylor: Man on Street, Eddie Levi Lee: Eddie, William J. White: Dave the Cook

Written by: Jeff Melvoin

Directed by: Michael Fresco

Holling enters Joel's office with a problem on his mind. He tells Joel that he hasn't paid taxes since 1959 and now owes to government nine thousand dollars. When Joel asks how he can help, Holling asks if he can get some kind of note to excuse him.

On Chris In The Morning, Chris receives a letter from his brother Bernard. Holling comes in very shy and uncomfortable. When Chris asks what's wrong, Holling tells him about his tax dilemma, and offers to sell him one-half interest in the Brick. Chris is thrilled and excited, realizing that he was born to run a bar..

In the Brick, Maurice storms in angry that no one in town is reading his newspaper, the Cicely News and World Telegram. Several people respond that the paper is terrible, and Maurice realizes that he needs more interesting material. As Chris stands behind the bar passing out free drinks, Holling stands idly by, feeling helpless at Chris's newfound control of the bar. Adam sits nearby, telling a wide assortment of farfetched stories to anyone who will listen, and Maurice is interested. After leaving, Maurice finds Adam walking home and offers him a position as a write on his paper. Adam is offended, and obviously paranoid that people will find out where he is. After some cajoling and an offer of money, Adam gives in.

A few days later, everyone in town is picking up Maurice's paper. The townspeople read raptly about trees in Alaska that actually make audible sounds, almost like talking. Maurice is thrilled by the success, but Joel tells him that no one will believe the story. At the same time, Maggie is walking through the woods, trying her best to hear the trees talking. She returns to town tells Joel that she could actually hear them. Joel blames it on the power of suggestion, but Maggie responds with evidences of plant intelligence. Meanwhile, Chris is passing out free pizza, a new item on the Brick's menu.

Maurice finds Adam and wants more material on the tree story. Adam relents, and begins dictating the article into Maurice's portable tape recorder. The next morning, Adam enters Maurice's house in a rage, telling him that he butchered Adam's story. Adam tells Maurice of his belief that everything that happens, everywhere, everyday, is monitored by the FBI and other unknown agencies. Maurice calls his beliefs paranoid. Adam replies by telling Maurice many intimate details of Maurice's life, such as the location of his birthmark, and his enamel replacement in his left lateral incisor. Maurice is stunned.

At Joel's office, Maggie wants to borrow a stethoscope so that she can hear the trees better. Joel finally snaps, and goes off to find Maurice. He tells Maurice that the public trust is at stake. Maurice, however, is ignorant, and can only see his newspaper's profits.

The next morning as the rain falls outside, Chris is sullen. He tries to announce some specials at the Brick over KBHR, but he looks over to see that it is nearly empty. He begins philosophizing about our need to own that which we love, and realizes that he is not happy owning a bar. Meanwhile, Holling is similarly depressed, and feels like he has to sell out the bar to Chris, since he can't be happy as just a partner. Holling finally goes over to see Chris, and Chris explains that he's unhappy and wants out. Holling is relieved, and says he will pay Chris back as soon as he can.

Maurice finds Adam, who has recently disappeared in the forest. In a moment of confrontation, Adam tells Maurice that it is all over. Maurice refuses to let the story die, and the two begin threatening each other with various means of bodily harm. Adam distracts Maurice momentarily, and vanishes into the forest. Returning to the Brick, he finds that things are back to normal and Joel tells him to get over it. Ed rushes in with another local newspaper that tells of a chemical spill in the forests which may have caused the trees to actually cry out in anguish. Maurice is more upset, now that he has found out that Adam was right after all.

That night, Maggie and Joel are walking through the forest and Maggie is trying to get Joel to hear the trees. Joel honestly tries to listen, and the episode ends with the two of them sitting on a log, facing away from each other, both trying desperately to hear something.

"Oy, Wilderness"

Guest Starring: Christine Elise: Cindy

Co-Starring: Peg Phillips: Ruth-Anne

Written by: Robin Green

Directed by: Miles Watkins

As Joel and Maggie are flying back from a vaccination, Joel is paranoid that the plane will crash. A malfunction occurs, and Joel begins screaming and praying as Maggie makes an emergency landing. They touch down in a nature preserve, days from where anybody will be able to reach them. Maggie is ready to face their situation, but Joel is fearful of visits by wild animals.

Back in town, a young woman arrives at the Brick and is looking for Shelly. The woman turns out to be Cindy, Shelly's friend from home. Cindy says that Wayne finally told her that he and Shelly were still married, even though Cindy and Wayne have been married for six months. Shelly is unwilling to get a divorce, since she's still resentful of the fact that Cindy stole her husband. After Shelly stops speaking to her, Holling finally sits down with Cindy and talks to her about her past with Shelly. Cindy complains to Holling about how she was always second to Shelly, and now Shelly won't even let go of Wayne whom she doesn't want anymore.

As Maggie is putting up the tent, Joel is sitting on the ground worrying about how they are going to eat. Maggie tells Joel to forget about the spoiled urban act, and Joel points out that he is out in the wilderness by coercion, and not by choice. Maggie is a little sympathetic, and trys to be more civil towards Joel. That night, as Maggie is asleep, Joel lies awake, starting at every sound he hears outside the protection of their tent. Finally, after Maggie's pleading, he lays down and attempts to get some rest.

ANSWERS ON PAGE 149

TRIVIA TEASERS: CHRIS

1) Where is Chris from?
a
2) What is Chris's birthday?

3) What was Chris's trade in prison?

4) What title does Chris hold?

5) How did Chris become ordained?

6) Who is Chris's half-brother?

7) What is Bernard's birthday?

8) Where is Bernard from?

9) How old was Chris's father when he died?

10) What was Chris's uncle's name?

11) How old was his uncle when he died?

12) What is the name of the lake that Chris lives by?

13) Who was Chris's first true love?

The next morning, Maggie begins work on her plane. Joel is unable to stomach the whale blubber which was given to them so Maggie goes to look for food. Before she goes off, she succumbs to Joel's whining, and gives him a pistol and a whistle to use if anything attacks while she's gone. As he tries to cook some seal liver over the campfire, he is practicing with a Spanish language tape. Suddenly, he hears sounds from the bushes, and begins frantically blowing the whistle only to see Maggie emerge. Maggie finds Joel's behavior childish, and barely tolerable.

Back in town, Cindy is busy performing hair makeovers and manicures for several townspeople. Shelly finally snaps from all the attention Cindy is getting, and the two engage in another argument. Eventually they cool down and discuss their respective roles in high school: Shelly, the perfect D-cup with seventeen-inch thighs, and Cindy, the second-rate friend who got to take all of Shelly's strays. After Cindy complains about her role, Shelly tells of the difficulty of always having to be perfect. The two end up crying and decide to forget their past arguments.

In a dream sequence, Maggie is a cavewoman attempting to cook a meal, while Joel is a caveman painting a hamburger on their wall. Maggie complains that Joel can not catch and kill food for their children, but then they become affectionate. In the tent,

Maggie and Joel begin kissing, but suddenly wake up and turn away from each other in shock.

The next morning, Maggie is stumped about her engine problems. Joel asks Maggie if the engine has valves, but Maggie rejects any of his suggestions. At Joel's insistent hunger, Maggie heads off in a rage, and goes off to kill something for them to eat. By the time she returns with a squirrel, her anger has subsided, and the two talk a little as the squirrel is roasting. Maggie tells Joel that she is almost ready to go off on her own to find a way back, certain that no one is coming to rescue them.

Back in Cicely, Shelly and Cindy convince Chris to perform a divorce for them over the radio. While Maurice and Holling stand witness, Shelly and Wayne, who is connected over the phone, denounce their vows for each other. Cindy thanks Shelly for being so kind, and then talks to Wayne on the phone.

As Maggie returns from an unsuccessful search expedition, she finds Joel deep in the work of repairing her engine. Maggie is livid, since she knows that Joel knows nothing about engines. Joel points out that the human heart has valves similar to an engine's, and he cleaned out one of the valves that appeared to be clogged. Maggie refuses to listen to his excuses, but finally consents to trying to start the aircraft one more time. The engine roars to life, and as Maggie sits, incredulous, Joel runs around screaming, "I did it! Me!!"

In front of the Brick, Cindy and Shelly say a tearful farewell, while Holling and Maurice watch in confusion. That night, Holling tells Shelly that if she really wants to leave, and go to be with her high school friends, he doesn't want to stop her. Shelly responds by telling Holling that from now on, she's going to make him feel young again.

"Our Tribe"

Co-Starring

Peg Phillips: Ruth-Anne, Rosetta Pintado: Gloria Noanuk

Featuring: Harry Pringle: Morning Star, Mary Waskey: Judy Baker, Al Hood: George Tuck, Katherine Davis: Libby Stevens, Frank Welker: Goat Sounds

Written by: David Assael

Directed by: Lee Shallat

Upon arriving in his office, Joel is surprised to find a goat in his waiting room. Marilyn tells him that it is a gift from Mrs. Noanuk, who Joel recently treated. Joel wants to return it and offers to give it to Marilyn. She won't accept it, saying it wouldn't be right. Later, at Joel's invitation, Mrs. Noanuk arrives at the office. Joel tells her that he has no rapport with animals, but she thinks that she insulted him, and that he deserves more. She tells him that she is going to adopt him and make him a member of the tribe. After Mrs. Noanuk leaves, Marilyn congratulates Joel, who is desperately looking for a way to get out of it. Marilyn tells him that he can't get out of it, and Joel is flustered.

At the Brick, Holling is in a cheerful mood, despite the fact that Shelly is gone to visit friends out of town for a few days. He is preparing to close up the Brick for a few days to wax the floors when Maggie delivers a package to him. She is suspicious because Holling is evasive about its contents. That night Holling kicks everyone out of the Brick, but Chris offers to stay and help him wax the floors. Holling refuses and quickly kicks Chris out.

At Joel's cabin, he sits watching the goat chew on one of his chairs. Ed enters and compliments him on the goat. Joel tells Ed that Marilyn is mad at him for not wanting to join the tribe. Ed tells Joel that Mrs. Noanuk is also upset at his refusal, and Joel begins to weaken. In town, he chases Marilyn down the street asking her why she won't speak to him. Marilyn stoically continues, and Joel admits that she has made an impression on him. He is desperate and upset, and finally tells her that he will allow himself to be adopted into the tribe. Marilyn smiles and walks off.

That night, Joel visits Mrs. Noanuk's house with Ed and Marilyn in tow. She informs him that in order to become a member of the tribe he has to give away everything. The next day, as Ed is boxing up Joel's belongings, Joel begins to see the value of such a symbolic act, to avoid rampant materialism. As Ed is about to leave, Joel asks him when he gets his stuff back. Ed stares blankly at Joel, explains that Mrs. Noanuk is in a different tribe than Ed, and quickly leaves.

Joel goes in to work and finds the Council of Elders waiting to meet him. He is cordial and introduces himself, and is pleased when they give him a bearskin vest to wear. When he enters his office however, he finds that his poster is missing. Angry at Marilyn, he asks her when it will stop, and she responds, "Now." Joel says he feels appropriately purged and chastened by the whole process, and Marilyn tells him that now he must fast.

Later that night, Ed visits Joel, and finds him drinking a home-made tribal tea, which is his only nourishment during the fast. Ed brings a box of stuff for Joel, but Joel soon discovers that everything that Ed brought isn't actually Joel's possessions, but poor substitutes. Joel throws a fit, and ends up sitting on the floor, finally giving up.

The next morning, Joel takes his goat for a walk and talks with Ed about tribal relations. Ed reminds Joel that he was adopted and was passed around a lot. Joel thinks about tribal relations and the contrast to his own tribe, the Jewish tribe. When he returns to work, he finds a crowd of people in his waiting room, playing checkers, playing music, and recreating since the Brick is still temporarily closed. Joel confronts Marilyn about his belongings, and she tells him that she never said that he'd get the same stuff back. Over the radio, Chris expresses his support for Joel in the flesh sacrifice to come. Joel runs in a panic over to KBHR to ask Chris what the sacrifice actually entails. Chris doesn't know, but is envious of Joel's adoption. Joel confides in Chris that he's only doing it to make Marilyn and Mrs. Noanuk happy, and Chris responds, "Sometimes it's hard to avoid the happiness of others."

Late that night Maggie enters the Brick through the back door and finds Holling studying star charts. Holling finally confesses to Maggie that he's not actually waxing the floors, but preparing to see a certain star, which will only be visible once more before vanishing forever. The star was one that he purchased years before to name after a dear friend of his, Eleanor. She is long dead but Holling wants to see her star one more time. However, despite his best efforts he is unable to find it. Maggie consoles him, and tells him that the present is the most important, not the past.

Chris is at KBHR late at night, playing the blues because the Brick is closed. Maurice enters and asks him what's wrong, and Chris decides to drive two hundred miles out to the Kicking Mule. In a touching moment of concern, Maurice offers to drive Chris in his Cadillac, and says that Chris can sit in the back and howl at the moon. The two leave with high spirits.

The next morning, Joel enters town for the ceremony accepting him into the tribe. Morning Star says a few words, and then Mrs. Noanuk announces that she has adopted Joel as her grandson. Joel steps up, genuinely appreciative, and for the first time actually seems happy. He thanks her, and she presents him with a plaque containing his Indian name. When the ceremony finishes Joel is exhilarated and everyone congratulates him. Joel has finally found a place where he belongs.

"Things Become Extinct"

Guest Starring

Bryson Liberty: Ira Wingfeather

Co-Starring: Peg Phillips: Ruth-Anne, Jerry Morris: Earl the Barber

Teleplay by: Robin Green

Story by: Mitchell Burgess

Directed by: Dean Parisot

As Ed delivers a package to the Brick, he tells Shelly about his newfound film project. He wants to capture on film some craft that is truly original, something that no one else can do. Shelly informs Ed that Holling's famous pies were actually taken from a recipe on the back of a box of Jell-O. Ed finally decides to film Joel, who is one of a vanishing breed of Jews. Joel is quick to inform Ed that Jews are far from being a vanishing breed and that there are plenty of Jews in Alaska.

For support, he looks in the phone book for North Tongas, a nearby town. He looks up the name Cohen, which is the Jewish equivalent of Smith. After being unable to find a single Cohen, he looks in the Fairbanks phone book, where he is only able to find one Cohen and three Greenbergs. Back at his office, he is looking through local phone directories for any Jewish names. He finally tracks down a town named Velachiske which he suspects would have some people of Jewish descent.

As Ed is working in Ruth-Anne's store replacing a light bulb, Ira Wingfeather walks in to give Ruth-Anne some duck flutes that he has made. He tells Ruth-Anne that the flutes are unique, and Ed looks up, just as the light bulb above his head turns off. After Ira leaves, Ed chases him out and they agree to begin filming the next day.

Holing is getting a shave when Maggie walks in to deliver a letter. Holling asks Maggie to read it to him, and she reads that Holling's uncle Charlie is dead. Holling is stunned, since his uncle was only one hundred and ten, which is still relatively young for a Vinceour male. When he returns to the Brick, he looks for a jug of homemade vodka to drink to Charlie's memory. When he finds it is all gone he is even more depressed.

Early the next morning, Ed shows up to Ira's trailer and begins filming as the two of them go off to look for a branch from which to make a duck flute. After they track down an appropriate branch, they return to the trailer, where Ira says he will let the wood rest until tomorrow, and Ed leaves.

The next morning, Chris is surprised to find rice being served at the Brick instead of hash browns. Shelly tells him that Holling left the night before and took all the potatoes with him. Chris realizes where Holling has gone and goes out to a run-down cabin in the middle of the woods. There, he finds Holling running a still and making a batch of "the good stuff." Holling is drinking heavily from a jug and tells Chris that life is passing by.

Chris joins him and the two discuss their respective mid-life crises. For Holling, whose family members usually live beyond one hundred ten, sixty-three is about mid-life. Chris's family doesn't live much beyond forty. In fact, Chris has absolutely no memory of the year between twenty-two and twenty-three. The entire year is simply one big blur. The two men sit alone and think.

At Ira's trailer, Ed begins filming again as Ira tells how he carves the duck flutes. After a while Ed stops filming and simply watches with rapt attention as Ira works his craft. Afterwards, Ira tells Ed that he is the last of his line, and after him, no one will be left who can make the duck flutes. Ed is bothered by this, and afraid to see something die off completely. Ira tells Ed that things become extinct and that change is inevitable.

On a winding mountain road, Maurice drives Joel out to find the town of Velachiske. They nearly pass by the town, which consists of a few run-down buildings by the roadside. After finding that the town has been abandoned for a long time, Joel feels even more depressed and alone.

Holling shows up to the Brick, obviously drunk, and looking for more potatoes for the still. When Shelly gets mad at him for getting so depressed, Holling lashes out at her, asking her what she knows about life anyway. Shelly is visibly hurt when reminded of their age difference, and tells Holling that she won't let him drag her down with him. She finds Joel in his office, and asks him what she should do about Holling. Joel promises to go talk to Holling out at the cabin. When he arrives, he finds Holling at work on his vodka, but Joel decides not to drink. After telling Holling what a great life he has, Holling tells Joel to look at his own life: he has no woman, no home, he's stuck in Cicely, and the best years of his life are draining. This strikes Joel, and from some combination of Holling's speech and his own personal feelings of loneliness, he takes a drink.

As Ed sits at home, watching his films of Ira making the duck flute, he watches with respect and awe. He suddenly realizes what he must do to keep Ira's life's work from dying off, and leaves to see Ira. When Ira opens the door, he is surprised to find Ed with all of the rolls of film. Ed gives him the film, and says that he wants to learn how to make the duck flutes. Ira smiles, evidently pleased, and invites Ed in for his first lesson.

That night, Joel and Holling are sleeping in the cabin. Marilyn shows up, awakens Holling, and tells him that it's time to go. Holling is confused, but follows Marilyn into town. When he arrives at the Brick, everyone is gone, and a single chair with his name on it sits in front of a large crate standing on end. A hole has been cut in the side of the crate, and as Holling sits, Shelly begins performing a puppet show about Holling's life. She tells of how Holling met Maurice, and how he fell in love with Shelly. Through the puppets, she tells Holling that she feels like the luckiest woman in the world, and Holling is in tears when she finishes. The two of them hug and walk upstairs to their room.

"Burning Down The House"

Guest Starring: Bibi Besch: Jane O'Connell, John M. Jackson: Larry Coe (Chimney Sweep)

Co-Starring: Peg Phillips: Ruth-Anne

Featuring: Gary Taylor: Gary, Haynes Brooke: Townsperson

Written by: Robin Green

Directed by: Rob Thompson

Out in a field by an old barn, Joel is talking with Chris while Chris is building something. Chris tells Joel that he plans on constructing a catapult to fling a cow, in order to create a "pure moment." Joel is left pondering this inhumane act.

On KBHR, Chris asks townspeople for some mechanical tools, along with a cow to fling. At Ruth-Anne's store, Maggie is buying supplies to prepare for her mother's visit. All the while, she complains to Ruth-Anne about her mother, who is "pathologically polite." Later, when she brings her mother into town, Maggie is obviously uncomfortable and constantly trying to please her mother. The two of them enter the Brick for lunch.

Inside, Joel is sitting at the bar, near a man whom Joel knows only as the chimney sweep, Bob. The man's identity puzzles Joel, who feels like he recognizes him. Under Joel's scrutiny, Bob leaves. As Maggie and her mother eat, and her mother complains about the food, Maggie discovers that her mother is visiting to tell Maggie that she is getting a divorce. Maggie is stunned by the revelation.

Back at Maggie's cabin, her mother is busy looking around and making small talk, while Maggie is anxious to discuss her parents' impending separation. Mrs. O'Connell calmly tells her that the papers have already gone through and they're just waiting for final approval. Maggie is told that her parents' marriage has been long dead, and that Mrs. O'Connell wants to finally go out and experience life. Despite her mother's convincing, Maggie is still unwilling to believe that her parents are getting a divorce.

On the way to Ruth-Anne's store, Chris runs into Gary, who offers Chris his cow. Entering Ruth-Anne's store, Chris finds Joel picking up his mail. When he opens his Golf Digest, something clicks inside Joel's mind, and he suddenly remembers Larry Coe, who missed a three-foot putt, and subsequently lost the Masters. Joel is convinced that Bob the chimney sweep is actually Larry Coe, who left professional golf shortly after the Masters. Joel is exhilarated by his discovery. Returning to his cabin, Joel confronts Bob, and tells him that he knows Bob's identity. Bob is visibly upset by Joel's information and leaves.

That night, Maggie leaves the Brick drunk and depressed over her mother's news. As she begins walking home, she is passed by several fire trucks, which are going to her house. Upon arriving at the blaze where her house once stood, Maggie finds her mother, who apologizes for having accidentally started the fire. Maggie's face is frozen with conflicting emotions.

The following day, Ed arrives at the barn to visit Chris, who is busy polishing an axe. Ed expresses admiration for Chris, and mentions the scene where a cow is flung in Monty Python and the Holy Grail. When he hears this, Chris suddenly stops his work, and slumps into a chair. He tells Ed that since it has already been done by Monty Python, it wouldn't be a pure moment. Ed leaves, sorry for his interference. He returns to the Brick, where Joel is telling Holling and Maurice about Larry Coe's past golfing career. Ed tells them that Chris has given up.

In town, Joel runs into Bob who is leaving Cicely to go to Greenland. Bob explains that he can't tolerate pity and that he feels like every time anyone looks at him they will see someone who

ANSWERS ON PAGE 149

TRIVIA TEASERS: ED

1) How was Ed found?

2, Who was his mother?

3, What was his father's name?

4, Where does his father live?

choked at the Masters. He drives off leaving Joel alone with his guilt.

Maurice enters Chris's barn to find Chris sitting alone thinking. Maurice admonishes him for giving up so soon, and Chris responds that repetition is the death of art, and inspiration doesn't grow on trees. Maurice ignores this and tells Chris that he is gutless for giving up. He tells Chris not to sit feeling sorry for himself, but to pick himself up and go on. Chris begins thinking about the dichotomy of creation and destruction and is inspired again.

Back in town, Chris shows up at Maggie's house, only to find her digging through the rubble. Maggie's mood worsens when she finds the melted remains of her dioramas, which were memorials to her dead boyfriends. Chris compares the burning of her house to the phoenix, which would rise from its own ashes and be reborn. He finds her charred piano, still out of tune, and Maggie agrees to let him use it. As she leaves the house, Chris plays an off-key version of "As Time Goes By."

Out near the woods, Bob is driving by when he spots Joel by the side of the road waving him down. Joel says that he feels bad and asks Bob to come with him into the forest. Bob reluctantly follows and comes upon an astroturf green set up to resemble the eighteenth hole at Augusta. Joel commentates as Bob resignedly putts the ball in. Afterwards, Bob remains unchanged, but Joel feels much better, and Bob departs.

Maggie goes to visit her mother at Maurice's house, bringing along a pair of shoes which miraculously survived the fire. After some superficial conversation about the shoes, Jane apologizes for ruining Maggie's life, and Maggie cries at the apology. When Mrs. O'Connell says she has to leave Cicely, Maggie honestly wants her to stay, and is able to forgive her mother.

Out in an open field, a crowd is gathered around an enormous device which is connected to something hidden underneath a cloth. As the townspeople look on, Chris makes a speech thanking Maurice for his inspirational talk, and Maggie for the shreds of her ruined home. He pulls out a sword, has Marilyn draw away the sheet, revealing the piano, and then activates the mechanism. The piano is launched in a high arc, and in a truly magical moment, seems to hang in the air while everyone watches. Its elegant tumbling is accompanied by "The Blue Danube Waltz". Finally, it crashes to the ground, earning gasps of appreciation from the onlookers. For a moment, even Maurice has a flash of comprehension, and Chris's face breaks into a self-satisfied smile.

"Democracy In America"

Guest Starring: Rita Taggart: Edna Hancock

Co-Starring: Peg Phillips: Ruth-Anne, Clayton Coraztte: George the Barber

Featuring: William J. White: Dave the Cook, Eric Ray Anderson: Customer, Dorothy Hanlin: Dorothy, Patrick Ryals: Logger

Written by: Jeff Melvoin

Directed by: Michael Katleman

Ed and Chris are in the Brick playing pool and talking with Holling. Edna Hancock enters and Holling is very friendly towards her. She tells Holling that it is too late for kindness. He appears genuinely confused, and she tells him that she is running against him for mayor, and walks out.

The next day, Chris is on KBHR, talking about the upcoming election and espousing democracy. Ed is in Joel's office, concerned about a facial tick, and stressed over the election, which will be the first in which he could vote. Joel, who never knew that Holling was mayor, is surprised to find that there has never been an election in Cicel because no one has ever challenged Holling's position. Later at the Brick, Holling says that he never asked to be mayor, and merely accepted the position because everyone wanted him to. Ed is asking Maggie's advice on who to vote for, which leads Joel and Maggie into an argument about political qualifications. The argument ends with Joel, a Republican, telling Maggie that there is nothing ennobling about being poor, and Maggie, a Democrat, calling Joel a self-serving materialistic pig.

Holling goes to visit Edna, and apologizes for not putting up the stop sign that she requested years ago. He offers to look into it, but Edna once again tells him that it is too late and asks him to leave. Later that day, while Holling is at the barber, he finds that many people may actually be considering voting for Edna. Having run unchallenged in the past, the thought of having to run the electoral race disturbs Holling, and he begins taking a hand in his own future.

At Ruth-Anne's store, Joel asks Ruth-Anne why everyone is making such a big deal about a minor election. Ruth-Anne explains that the election is a big event in Cicely. After appraising his keen political intellect, she appoints him election commissioner, threatening to remove his credit line if he refuses. Joel soon discovers that his partner is Maggie, the chairman of the election committee.

Joel and Maggie are in Joel's office discussing the upcoming election. Joel considers the results of the election pointless, but finds the demographics of the process interesting. In fact, he admits that he used to memorize election statistics like other kids memorized baseball cards. Maggie, on the other hand, feels that the emotion is the most important, and is concerned about how the polling place looks, to create the proper mood. Holling shows up to see Marilyn, and asks her how the Indian people are planning to vote. Marilyn is quiet, as usual, and tells Holling that an individual's vote is personal.

On Chris In The Morning, Chris again discusses the concept of the election, and embarks on an extended monologue about the democratic process. Outside, he meets Ed, who is studying political concepts. Chris admits to Ed that, having been a convicted felon, he can no longer vote. Ed, who has only recently begun to exercise his right to vote, is sympathetic.

At Holling's bar, he is giving away free beer to all the patrons. Edna and Ruth-Anne come in and tell him to stop, as his gifts are a violation of election regulations. Holling is upset again, and tells Maurice that he no longer simply wants to beat Edna, he now wants to destroy her. Meanwhile, Maggie is trying to figure out how to decorate the debate area, a process which Joel considers pointless. Maggie compares their arguments to the election, which she believes is about Woman vs. Man.

On election day, Maggie and Joel are making last-minute changes to the polling place. The two compliment each other warmly, and then let the voters in. Chris gives a voice-over as slow-motion shots of voters are shown. The cheerful music builds until Chris arrives, dressed up, cleanly shaven, and with a neat haircut. He is hardly recognizable as the long-haired, unshaven DJ seen before. Although he can not vote, he has come to watch democracy in action.

That night, Chris is drained, and delivers the election results over the radio, announcing Edna as the winner by eight votes. At the Brick, Holling is annoyed by his loss, but is slowly coming to terms with it. When Edna enters, Holling buys her a drink in friendship.

As Joel and Maggie walk home from the polling place, they congratulate each other on a successful election, and Joel offers to buy Maggie dinner. She agrees with a smile, and they enter the

Brick together, as Chris once again declares the success of democracy.

"The Three Amigos"

Guest Starring: Joanna Cassidy: Solvang Planey, Norbert Weisser: Reinhard Shoulder

Co-Starring: Peg Phillips: Ruth-Anne

Featuring: Brian T. Finney: Teak, Tom Spiller: Pig Eye

Written by: Mitchell Burgess and Robin Green

Directed by: Matthew Nodella

Holling and Shelly are working in the Brick late one night, when Maurice enters with a solemn air. He tells Holling that Bill Planey is dead. As Shelly asks who Bill Planey is, Holling tells Maurice that they will leave at first light, and the two men leave to make preparations.

The next morning, Holling is purchasing supplies at Ruth-Anne's store, as they prepare to go bury Bill out at No-Name Point. The two plan to go out to Bill's cabin, pick up the body, and then ride out on horseback to bury him. Ed shows up with a coffin, and Maurice and Holling put two horses into a trailer, climb into the truck, and drive off. As they depart, Chris watches them, and begins his radio reading of Call of the Wild by Jack London.

Down the road somewhere, the trailer gets a flat tire, and they stop to fix it. Holling's back suddenly goes out, and he is unable to help. While Maurice works, the two men reminisce about their exploits with Bill. Over a campfire that night, they both consider their decision to lead more domestic lives. Holling says that part of him is still out there in the wilderness, and they sleep.

The next day, the two men ride to Bill's cabin with their supplies on a litter attached to one of the horses. Upon arriving, they are surprised to find Solvang Planey, who was Bill's wife. Neither of them had known that he had a wife, and they are equally surprised to find his body twice the size they expected. They realize that the coffin will be too small. Solvang cooks them dinner, and they realize why Bill gained so much weight.

Chris's reading of Call of the Wild is given as a voice-over to Maurice and Holling's activity, and is often similar. When Chris reads about Skeet setting her sights on Buck, Solvang approaches Holling, who is working on the coffin. Solvang begins hitting on him, but Holling quickly explains about his relationship. Solvang thinks he is a fool and leaves. The next morning, when the men prepare to leave, Solvang announces that she is coming along and hops behind Maurice on his horse. Maurice and Holling exchange an annoyed glance, and the three ride off.

In camp that night, Solvang sneaks into Maurice's bag with him and tries to kiss him. Maurice is completely uncomfortable, and concerned by Bill's body which is so nearby. Solvang is annoyed by his squeamishness, and goes back to her own sleeping bag. The next morning, they awake to find the horses gone, and as Maurice and Holling argue, Chris reads about a fight among the dogs.

They finally track the horses down at Two Forks, a small bar sitting by itself. Solvang is pleased to find that the wife of the proprietor, Reinhard Shoulder, left him weeks before, and she eyes him like a predator. Meanwhile, Maurice and Holling play a game of bridge with two men. They end up in a fight and barely emerge triumphant. They prepare to leave, and Solvang announces her intentions to stay with Reinhard. The two men are confused and ride off with Bill in tow.

As they ride along the edge of a river, Holling's horse rears up and Bill's body goes sliding down the slope into the river. The two men follow it and manage to catch it, although the salt in which it was packed is beginning to leak out. That night, Maurice is fearful of frostbite and Bill's body is beginning to ripen. They finally decide to bury Bill by the river, rather than risk a trip to No-Name Point with few supplies. The next morning they bury him, say a few words over the grave, and then head back.

In Cicely, they are greeted warmly by their friends as Chris talks about the longing for the wild. As Holling recounts the story of their trip to Shelly, music begins playing and a montage of scenes from the episode is shown. The uniqueness of this episode, which focuses almost solely on two characters is elegant and offers a welcome change of pace from earlier episodes.

"Lost And Found"

Guest Starring: Valerie Mahaffey: Eve, Time Winters: Emile, Noble Willingham: Colonel Gordon McKern

Co-Starring: Peg Phillips: Ruth-Anne, Featuring: William J. White: Dave the Cook, Gary Taylor: Mr. Swanson, Robert J. Zenk: Patron

Written by: Diane Frolov and Andrew Schneider

Directed by: Steve Robman

Late at night, Joel is in his cabin writing a letter to a friend from medical school. He tells his friend about how much he enjoys the pure, elemental life in Alaska. Joel believes himself lucky to have the silence and the darkness around him, but is rather unconvincing is his praises of Alaska. Even as he writes, he looks around worriedly, pick up a golf putter defensively, and continues the letter.

In his office the next morning, Joel asks Marilyn if she can explain the weird, almost human sounds he heard in his cabin last night. Marilyn has no explanation that can ease Joel's mind. Just then, Eve walks in, and after she refuses to leave, Joel agrees to give her a complete medical workup.

At the Brick, Maurice is telling Shelly and Ed about Colonel Gordon McKern, Maurice's former commanding officer who is coming to visit him in Cicely. Maurice is obviously respectful of the Colonel, who, Maurice says, never took anything from anyone. Joel enters and sits down, asking more people about the strange voice he heard last night. Holling and Ruth-Anne exchange glances, and the tell Joel that the voice must have been Jack, who killed himself in the cabin long ago.

In a garage, Maggie is fixing her truck when Joel walks in. He complains to Maggie about Jack, angry that she never told him anything about it. Maggie says that she forgot, but she obviously feels a bit ashamed at not telling Joel. When prodded, she finally tells Joel the circumstances of Jack's death, including the fact that after he shot himself, he crawled over to the wall and wrote "Alone, alone" in his own blood. Joel is disturbed by this information, though he still steadfastly professes not to believe in ghosts. Finally, Maggie sincerely apologizes for misleading Joel, but he wants her to do something about it.

That night, Joel and Ed are playing gin in Joel's cabin. Ed finally gets tired and prepares to leave, but Joel wants him to stay, since it is only 1:30. When asked about ghosts, Ed tells Joel that they usually hang around when they have unfinished business. He tells Joel to ask himself why Jack would be trying to warn him, and then when Joel is completely spooked, Ed leaves.

The next day, Maurice brings Colonel McKern into the Brick to meet everyone and Maurice is obviously trying to impress the Colonel. Meanwhile, Joel is in his office having been awake all night worried about Jack. Marilyn tells him that Jack never hurt anyone, which is small comfort to Joel. He spots Maggie outside, and tells her that she needs to give him a new cabin. She says that she has none available, but after Joel presses, she says she will see what she can do.

Back in Joel's office, he finds Eve acting as secretary, keeping herself busy until her test results come in. A patient who came in while Joel was out is in the examining room, and Eve has already prepared a preliminary diagnosis. Joel is bothered by this breach ·of etiquette, but is less angry when her workup turns out to be completely accurate.

Maurice and the Colonel are out fishing on the edge of a lake, when the Colonel mentions a lodge he is opening up in Montana. He tells Maurice of the difficulty he has had raising investment capital, and asks Maurice if he would like to invest $60,000. Maurice is quiet, but nonetheless agreeable to putting up the money. The Colonel, however, appears very uncomfortable asking. When the men return to Maurice's cabin, he writes out the check, while McKern makes a feeble attempt to start some light conversation. Maurice is quiet, obviously stricken with the mortality he now sees in Colonel McKern.

At Ruth-Anne's store, Joel asks to see the town records to find out some information about Jack. Ruth-Anne has a box of personal effects taken from the cabin and as Joel pores through them, he finds that Jack was a person very similar to Joel. Joel is unable to find a reason why the man would kill himself, and Ruth-Anne leaves him alone to read about Jack.

That night, Joel has taken Jack's belongings home with him, and is looking them over when Maggie walks in with Emile, who is there to exorcise the ghost. Joel asks where Jack will go once he is exorcised, and Emile informs him that Jack will probably wind up below, since suicide is a mortal sin. Joel feels uncomfortable about being the cause of Jack's eternal torment and quickly shuffles Emile out.

As Eve enters the next day, Joel informs her that her symptoms are real and that she is pregnant. She is understandably surprised, but when Joel suggests that they schedule a prenatal exam, Eve thanks Joel for his help and informs him that he's not qualified to be her obstetrician. Joel is stunned as Eve walks out. Soon after Maurice comes in and his Cadillac is seen outside being towed, the front-end smashed in. Maurice tells Joel that he was so flustered because the Colonel asked him for money, that he lost control of the car, and drove it into a tree. Joel fails to see the importance of this act, but Maurice is obviously overwhelmed with a new view of Colonel McKern.

Maggie enters the Brick just as Holling is closing up and finds Joel sitting alone at a table reading more about Jack. After hearing a few pieces of personal information from Joel, Maggie informs him that he and Jack are one and the same. Maggie points out that Jack had no friends, to which Joel claims that he has lots of friends. When he asks Holling if they are friends, Holling says that Joel always kept to himself, and made sure that people knew he wasn't permanently staying in Cicely. Maggie leaves, and Joel is left thinking about his past attitudes towards the town. This is a monumental moment of self-realization where Joel has an opportunity to change his entire attitude toward the people of Cicely.

The following morning, Maurice escorts the Colonel to his flight, and McKern tells Maurice that he didn't turn down the space program, he was just never asked. Maurice looks at the man with a newfound sense of respect and they part ways.

At Joel's cabin, he is throwing a party, and cooking burgers for everyone. Maggie asks him why he has suddenly changes his attitude, and Joel tells her that maybe the town isn't so bad after all. Eve is talking to Shelly and Marilyn about her baby, Maurice is telling Ruth-Anne about Colonel McKern, and Holling gathers everyone together for a group photo. At the flash, the scene returns to Chris at KBHR, late at night. He has the picture hanging on his wall, and as he talks about the role of friendship, the camera pans across each character in turn, while the sounds of laughter from the party can be heard. The final shot is of Maggie and Joel, sitting together, with their faces frozen in a moment of laughter.

"My Mother, My Sister"

Guest Starring: Wendy Schaal: Tammy Tambo, Sean O'Bryan: Kenny Cadashay, Adam Arkin: Adam

ANSWERS ON PAGE 149

ANSWERS ON PAGE 149

TRIVIA TEASERS: MARILYN

1) What is Marilyn's cousin's name?

2) What is Leonard's profession?

3) How long has Leonard Quinhagak been practicing medicine?

Co-Starring: Peg Phillips: Ruth-Anne, William J. White: Dave the Cook

Written by: Kate Boutilier and Mitchell Burgess

Directed by: Rob Thompson

Joel's rush of morning patients ends with a baby left alone in a car seat in his waiting room. Marilyn did not see the mother, and all that is left with the baby is a diaper bag. Marilyn hands the baby to Joel and goes to get talcum powder. Ed and Joel examine the baby who appears to be healthy. Joel ponders about the kind of person who would simply abandon a baby, and Ed reminds him that he himself was abandoned as a child.

In the Brick's kitchen, Adam gets upset at Dave's lack of cooking ability. Holling chastises him for yelling at Dave, saying that no one is forcing him to work there. Adam mentions that he needs the money to support the baby, but is sincerely apologetic and goes back in to work with Dave. On KBHR, Chris puts out an announcement about the baby, along with a request for names. Inside the Brick, Shelly is surprised when Tammy shows up to tell Shelly that she got engaged. Tammy looks every bit as young as Shelly, and asks even more irresponsible. Holling is understandably surprised when Shelly introduces Tammy as her mother.

Upstairs in Shelly's room, Tammy is excited as she tells Shelly about how she met her fiance, Kenny, at a Desert Storm parade. After they get married, the two of them are planning to live in San Diego. Shelly is just as excited as Tammy. Later that night, Maurice and Holling watch appreciatively as Tammy dances as Holling holds the baby. Maurice had met Tammy before, as Shelly's talent coach at the Miss Northwest Passage pageant. He mentions that he though that Tammy was her sister. Shelly is a bit uncomfortable at this comparison, but Holling does not notice.

Outside the Brick, Joel compliments Adam on his cooking and Adam thanks him. Joel immediately knows something is wrong, because Adam is usually rude to everyone. Adam mentions that he feels weird, and almost happy. Adam is apparently very concerned about this, for he is not himself anymore. He walks away, feeling that something's wrong.

The next day, Kenny enters the Brick and looks very young. He meets Holling, but Holling is confused when he refers to Shelly as Tammy's sister. After Tammy arrives and greets Kenny, the four of them sit down to talk. Holling talks about the natural wonder of a local sinkhole, but Tammy and Kenny look politely uninterested. Meanwhile, Tammy and Kenny talk with Shelly about Slash and Guns 'n' Roses, a conversation in which Holling is lost. Later, as Tammy is preparing for bed, Shelly vents her rage complaining that she always has to act as Tammy's older sister. She threatens to tell Kenny that Tammy is actually her mother and walks out in a rage.

At Joel's cabin, he arrives to find Adam cleaning house. Joel attributes this to Couvaid Syndrome, or sympathetic pregnancy, where the man experiences the same pregnancy experience as the woman. Adam is doubtful, but can offer no other explanation for his condition. The next day, Adam arrives again and blends formula for the baby. Joel attributes this to the hormones released during the second trimester of pregnancy. Adam eventually leaves to see his wife, satisfied with his role as chef, husband, and father.

That afternoon, Kenny is worried when he is unable to find Tammy anywhere. Shelly finds an apologetic note left by Tammy and eventually finds her sitting alone in the movie theatre. Tammy apologizes for never having been a real mom for Shelly, but Shelly tells her that she was always proud. They finally resolve their past arguments, and Tammy promises to tell Kenny about their age differences.

At Joel's office, he finds Marilyn playing solitaire. When he asks about the baby, Marilyn tells him that the mother returned and picked it up. Joel is more than a little saddened by this discovery, and finds a pacifier in his office, which he holds tenderly.

"Wake-Up Call"

Guest Starring: Graham Greene: Leonard Quinhagak, Andreas Wisniewski: Arthur

Co-Starring: Peg Phillips: Ruth-Anne, William J. White: Dave the Cook, Robert Nicholson: Customer

Written by: Diane Frolov and Andrew Schneider

Directed by: Nick Marck

Holling is celebrating springtime by serving breakfast any time of the day for free. Maurice however, is suddenly disgusted by the same old coffee. He tells Holling to open his eyes to all the other kinds of coffee available and marches out. Meanwhile, Chris's allergies predict the onset and he announces the spotting of a brown bear at the corner of Spruce and Main. Maurice comes in and complains about Chris playing the same old music as always. Clearly, there is something deeply unsettled about Maurice.

In Joel's examining room, Shelly is visiting because of a mild rash. She attempts to make small talk with Joel, who merely responds with polite uncaring. Shelly remarks that Joel seems mad, but Joel explains that he is merely trying to distance himself from the patient so he can make a proper diagnosis. He concludes that she has dishpan hands, and advises her to put some cream on them.

At the Brick, Maggie is reading Ed a letter from her old high school friend, Elizabeth Schroeder, formerly Elizabeth Carrey. Elizabeth has just had a six pound, nine ounce baby boy, and Maggie is suddenly aware of her own loneliness. She thinks that since she never met anyone, she'll have to wait for the wave of divorces.

In Joel's office, he is visited by Leonard Quinhagak, an Indian healer who has arrived to observe Joel so he can get some ideas of conventional medicine. Joel confides in Leonard that his practice is extremely boring, then goes off to talk with Marilyn, who arranged the visit. She said that she asked Joel while he was playing Gameboy, and Joel contests that it was an unfair thing to ask. Nevertheless, Joel agrees to let Leonard watch.

Climbing into bed, Shelly finds the sheets scratchy, and when Holling touches her even slightly, she recoils in pain. Although she is wearing gloves to protect her hands, the rash has seemed to spread to other parts of her body. When she wakes up, she screams as she sees that she is peeling all over her body. Holling cannot believe his eyes.

Late at night, Maggie is watching television, and hears a noise outside. Going out with her gun, she finds a few overturned garbage cans. The next morning Chris announces her sighting over the radio as a warning about bears. Later the next day Maggie is driving near the forest and her truck gets stuck in the mud. A tall muscular man with long blond hair walks out of the woods and pushes her car as she accelerates, enabling her to leave. She thanks him quickly as she drives off and sees him watching her in her rearview mirror.

Shelly shows up at Joel's office, and Joel has trouble making a diagnosis. Leonard, however, makes small talk with Shelly, making her more at ease. Joel is upset by Leonard's interference, and finally prescribes cortizone for Shelly. After she leaves, Leonard asks unusual questions about Shelly's personal life and Joel doesn't know the answers. Leonard says that he spends hours, even days, talking with patients and is amazed that Joel can make a diagnosis so quickly. It is evident that his compliment is also a thinly veiled insult.

That night Maggie hears her garbage cans being overturned once again. As she leaves her house to check, the man who helped her earlier walks by, saying he recognized her truck. He tells Maggie that maybe the bear is looking for her, a comment which leaves Maggie flattered and a little confused. He introduces himself as Arthur but doesn't accept when Maggie invites him in. Just before he leaves, he tells Maggie that she has beautiful eyes, and she glows at the compliment.

Again, Shelly comes in to visit Joel, but Joel is gone. However, she sees Leonard, and they begin talking. She tells him a story about an egg she took care of once, and Leonard compares the hatching of the egg to Shelly's current rash, saying that she's shedding her skin. Shelly is cheered by this concept, and leaves in a much happier mood.

Out in the woods, Maggie spots Arthur standing in the river. As she looks on, he catches a fish out of the water with his bare hands. He tells Maggie that he lives alone, and carries her across the river to his home, a cave out on the middle of the forest. He has drinks set out, as if he were expecting her. They drink mead, which Arthur makes himself, and then they dance. Maggie is profoundly content, and Arthur tells her that he saw her one day in her plane, and he knew what was missing from his life.

At Maurice's house, Ed and Maurice are cleaning out his attic. Maurice comes upon an old set of bagpipes that his grandfather used to play and is moved by the memory. Meanwhile, Joel returns to his office, livid at Leonard's diagnosis to Shelly. Leonard explains that he could be wrong, and nothing is certain. He also tells Joel that his practice is boring because he is boring, and he should try to obtain a better demeanor toward his patients. Joel is angry and insulted by Leonard's criticism. Leonard says that being angry is better than being boring, and leaves.

Joel is curious when Maggie offers to fix anything that's wrong with his cabin and is surprised when she calls him "Joel," instead of "Fleischman". Joel heads over to the Brick and finds that Shelly's rash has completely gone away. He considers Leonard's words, and goes to visit him later at Marilyn's house. He tells Leonard how he never got along with patients, until he diagnosed a patient that no one else could, and saved his life. Joel thanks Leonard for reminding him of that feeling, and Leonard smiles.

Maggie returns to the cave to visit Arthur, only to find the cave cleaned out. As she leaves, she spots a brown bear, who looks at her for a moment in recognition, then leaves. She considers for a moment that the bear was Arthur.

As Chris reads about the beauty of springtime, we are treated to a montage of everyone's activities: Maggie is sitting on a log by the river, staring forlornly out into the distance; Holling and Shelly are sharing a bath; Marilyn is doing her gardening; Ruth-Anne is getting her hair done; Ed is hitting flies out in a field, a bucket of baseballs at his side; Joel is laughing as he talks to a patient; and Maurice is on his roof, playing his bagpipes to the late evening sun.

"The Final Frontier"

Guest Starring: Doug Ballard: Ron, Don R. McManus: Erick, Akemi Namei: Tourist #1, Rob Narita: Tourist #2

Co-Starring: Peg Phillips: Ruth-Anne Miller

Featuring: William J. White: Dave the Cook, Paul Fleming: Bar Patron #1, Wally Dalton: Bar Patron #2

Written by: Jeffrey Vlaming

Directed by: Tom Moore

In the Brick, Ed enters as Holling is in the middle of a joke. After Holling finishes, Ed tells him that Jesse is dead, and Holling's mood darkens immediately. Shelly asks who Jesse is, and Ed tells her that Jesse was a bear. When Holling and Ed go out to check on the bones, Holling confirms that they are Jesse's and that he died of natural causes. Although they were mortal enemies, Holling is sad at Jesse's passing.

Chris announces over KBHR that the Aurora Borealis is coming up, and he notices a group of Japanese tourists visiting town. They go by Maurice's office, and Maurice discovers that they are admirers of his astronautical exploits. Maurice is annoyed, and a little condescending, but still polite. He is shocked to find that they are staying at the inn run by Ron and Erick, whom Maurice knows to be homosexuals, a lifestyle of which he deplores.

Maggie shows up at Ruth-Anne's store with a package addressed to Richard McWilliams. No one knows of such a person, and Maggie, Marilyn, Ruth-Anne, and Ed all try to figure out what it could be. Meanwhile, Ron and Erick visit Maurice, and ask him to speak for the tourists at their hotel. Maurice is unwilling because of their sexual preference. However, as the men raise their offer and Maurice continues to refuse, they appear more amused than bothered.

The next day, Holling enters the Brick to find that Ed and Milt and the guys have reconstructed Jesse's skeleton in the middle of the bar. Holling can only stand in awe of Jesse's magnificence. At the same time, Maurice relents to give some tourists a tour of his house. When they see the picture of his Korean son, they begin laughing, but Maurice asks all of them to step outside, and they quickly apologize. After their cajoling, he finally decides to speak at the inn.

Maggie enters Joel's office carrying the package, and asks Joel to x-ray it. Joel refuses, citing laws against tampering with the mail. Again, Maggie is upset at Joel's inhuman lack of curiosity. However, she is able to get an x-ray from airport security, and Joel gives his own diagnosis about the contents of the box. Ruth-Anne decides to call a town meeting to decide whether or not to open the box.

At the Brick, Holling is packing supplies when Shelly comes downstairs. Holling tells Shelly that he needs to look for Jesse in Widowmaker's Cave, but Shelly is worried and scared. Holling tells her that it's something that he has to do, and leaves.

At the town meeting, Shelly presides as the former mayor's almost-wife. Joel goes on the record saying that he is against opening the package, and Chris comes out in support of him. Maggie says that she will take the risk, and Chris supports her as well. Chris finally breaks into a long-winded speech about the price of knowledge, and they finally agree to open the package. When they do, they find castanets, sunglasses, a boomerang, wooden shoes, I-Ching coins, and much more. There is also a letter from Richard McWilliams, dated June 8, 1988.

Richard sent the package to go where he could not, since he is only eight years old. The recipient is instructed to put something of his own into the package, and then forward it someplace far away. After an arduous argument, they finally decide to put in Joel's thermometer, which has been in the mouths of everyone in Cicely.

As Maurice gives his speech about his NASA experiences to the tourists, the Northern Lights begin. They all run quickly upstairs, leaving Maurice hanging in the middle of his speech. Ron and Erick inform Maurice that the tourists believe that by conceiving a child under the Northern Lights, the child will be gifted. Maurice is stunned, but concedes the men's good business sense.

Holling returns to the Brick completely worn out and somewhat injured. He informs Shelly that Jesse is in Widowmaker's cave, and in the forest and under the ocean, and in outer space. Jesse is always around the corner, and we have to be wary of where we step, in case we run into him. Nevertheless, Holling is exhilarated, and goes upstairs with Shelly. Ruth-Anne hands the newly-sealed package to Maggie which they send off to Barwana, India, a place that Ed randomly picked off the globe.

"It Happened In Juneau"

Guest Starring: Richard Cummings Jr.: Bernard Stevens, Beth Broderick: Linda Angelo

Co-Starring: Peg Phillips: Ruth-Anne

Featuring: Woody Eney: Hotel Clerk, Peter Bradshaw: John Harcourt, John Billingsley: Patient, James Marsters: Bellhop, Kent Maclachlan: Dr. Paul Brennan

Teleplay by: David Assael and Robert Rabinowitz

Story by: David Assael

Directed by: Michael Katleman

On Chris In The Morning, Chris announce that Joel will be leaving on a weekend trip to Juneau for a medical conference. Suddenly, Chris's sentences begin to get jumbled up. Chris confusedly turns off the microphone and stops broadcasting.

Joel is in his office talking about finding available, single, female pediatricians at the conference. He is obviously looking forward to hooking up with someone in his own perceived social class. When he goes to catch his private flight, he discovers that Maggie is flying him instead of Red, since Maggie wants to see the touring company of Les Mis in Juneau.

At KBHR, Maurice asks Chris what is wrong and Chris has trouble answering. Almost immediately after, Chris's half-brother Bernard drives up, having returned from Africa. But when they greet each other, they are no longer mentally connected; Chris is thirsty, while Bernard is hungry. They go off to the Brick in confusion.

In Juneau, Joel and Maggie find that due to a water leak, several of the rooms are under water and they're forced to stay in a suite together for the weekend. Joel is not happy with the situation, but agrees as long as Maggie promises to keep her distance if he has guests. That night, as they prepare for their respective social events, Maggie comments on Joel's intended purpose to "bag some bimbos."

Joel merely tells her to make sure that they don't run into each other. At the conference, Joel foregoes the idle conversation with a male doctor, in favor of hunting down a prospective female. He is approached by a woman named Linda, who bluntly says that she'd prefer to skip past the idle chatter and get right to intercourse. Joel is a bit intimidated by her though, and makes an excuse to leave. She catches up to him later, and apologizes for coming on so strong. Joel makes another excuse, and Linda hints at his possible impotence before finally leaving him alone.

At the Brick, Bernard is showing the townspeople some of his slides of Africa. Chris, who is normally in sync with Bernard, guesses every slide wrongly. Later, as Bernard talks with Ruth-Anne, she comments on the half-moth encased in amber that he wears on a necklace. Bernard tells of the man who sold it to him and told him that he was destined to have it.

Late that night Joel is alone in his hotel room watching television when Maggie bursts in rather clumsily with a gentleman in tow. She is a little drunk and apologizes to Joel. The two retire to Maggie's bedroom and Joel goes to sleep. The next morning over breakfast Joel asks Maggie whether or not they slept together and Maggie finally admits that they did not. His jealousy is apparent, although he makes a feeble attempt to hide it.

That night Joel is stuck after the conference making small talk with the bellboy. Linda tracks him down again and invites him up to her room. He leaves the offer open, but ends up retiring to his room. Maggie shows up a bit later and says that she returned because she wanted to be with Joel, thinking he'd be alone. Joel asks if she'd like to go to dinner, and as Joel reaches for his coat they lock in an intense kiss. They agree to get ready and meet back in the middle of Maggie's bed. But when Joel eventually shows up, Maggie is fast asleep, the result of thirty-six hours of sleep deprivation. Joel tries to wake her and frustrated, returns to his own room.

That night Chris and Bernard sleep in Chris's trailer and dream of Africa. However, while Chris dreams of the body and feet of a giraffe, Bernard only gets the neck and head. They suddenly wake up, and start discussing the half-dream they experienced. Bernard makes the connection with the half-moth, because the moth is supposed to represent the soul in many cultures. He gives the moth to Chris, who begins speaking normally once again.

ANSWERS ON PAGE 149

TRIVIA TEASERS: RUTH-ANNE

1) What is Ruth-Anne's last name?

2) How old is Ruth-Anne?

3) When did Ruth-Anne come to Cicely?

4) What was Ruth-Anne's husband's name?

5) What are the names of her two sons?

6) What does Rudy do?

7) What does Matthew do?

The next morning Joel and Maggie have coffee and Joel brings up the the previous night. Before Joel gets a chance to complain about Maggie falling asleep, Maggie begins talking about how wonderful it was. Joel realizes that Maggie doesn't remember anything that happened, and is trying to cover it up assuming that they had sex. Joel plays with her a little bit, pretending to be disappointed with her performance. She is clearly uncomfortable at not being able to remember anything.

When they arrive back in Cicely, Joel is about to tell her the truth about what happened. But once again, Maggie interrupts him, and asks that he not tell anyone about what happened. As Joel listens in amazement, Maggie explains how embarrassed she would be if anyone found out that they had slept together. Joel agrees to forget it ever happened, although he knows it never actually did. He is understandably angry about her attitude towards him, and does not reveal to her the fact that they didn't have sex. They leave on very shaky terms, and it is apparent that there is trouble in the near future for the two of them.

"The Wedding"

Guest Starring: Valerie Mahaffey: Eve, Richad CUmmings Jr.: Bernard Stevens, Diane Delano: Officer Barbara Semanski, Adam Arkin: Adam

Co-Starring: Peg Phillips: Ruth-Anne, Ralph P. Martin: Ivory Springer

Featuring: William J. White: Dave the Cook

Written by: Diane Frolov and Andrew Schneider

Directed by: Nick Marck

While Joel is in his office reading, Adam and Eve suddenly show up and ask to have blood tests taken. When Joel asks why, Adam tells him that they need the tests to get married. Joel is confused thinking that they are already married.

Chris once again finds that his brother Bernard has come to visit, except this time he is passing through on his way to Russia. The two go over to the Brick, where Joel is just arriving. He sits near Maggie, who greets him nervously, before excusing herself and leaving in a hurry. Joel is confused by her attitude and talks to Marilyn who is busily making origami cranes for the wedding. After a long discussion, Shelly convinces Eve to let her be the maid of honor at the wedding.

Later that day Eve catches up to Joel on the street where he tells her that the blood tests have come out fine. She is not satisfied and asks Joel to run more tests. Just then, Maggie walks around the corner and stops in her tracks when she sees Joel. She smiles, says hi, and quickly leaves again. Eve chastises Joel for sleeping with her, an event which she heard of from Adam. Joel tries to convince Eve that he didn't actually sleep with Maggie, but Eve won't listen.

Seriously bothered by Maggie's attitude, Joel shows up to her door that night where he has to practically force his way in. Joel asks her what is wrong and Maggie insists that nothing is going on. Joel sits next to her, but she immediately jumps up and moves to another chair. Finally, Joel tells her that they never slept together. At first, Maggie is disbelieving and turns enraged.

The next day Adam and Eve meet Chris at the church to discuss the format for the wedding. In the middle of the discussion, Eve feels sharp pains like she is going into premature labor. At Joel's office, Eve is ready to call off the wedding but Joel reassures her that it is not premature labor that she is experiencing. For whatever reason, Eve obviously wants to get out of the wedding.

Joel is shopping at Ruth-Anne's store later that day when Maggie walks in. Joel tries to talk to her. After repeated apologizes, she finally asks Joel why he didn't sleep with her. This response takes Joel completely by surprise, and he explains that she fell asleep. Maggie is bothered by the fact that she didn't arouse enough passion in him to make him wake her up. Joel explains that he also has self-control. Maggie is offended that she inspires self-control in men, and storms off leaving Joel in a wake of confusion.

That night Joel complains to Holling and Maurice about women, while Maggie does the same with Ruth-Anne about men. Maggie explains to Ruth-Anne that she had this incredibly erotic fantasy worked out involving Joel. Her anger comes from the fact that the pleasure never actually transpired. Ruth-Anne tells her that if she's going to feel the guilt, she might as well experience the pleasure. Maggie suddenly brightens, as she realizes what she must do.

Maggie shows up to Joel's cabin and tells him that they should finish what they started in Juneau. By now, Joel is completely confused but accepts her affections as real. They begin kissing and Maggie asks Joel if he would let anything stand in his way of having her. He tells her that nothing could possibly stop him, not earthquakes, floods, or tidal waves. Suddenly, Maggie smiles happily, and realizes that she finally got Joel to really want her. Satisfied with this, she tells Joel that she no longer needs the actual sex part. Joel begins insisting, but Maggie stops him by thanking him for making her so happy and leaves.

The next day everyone in town shows up for the wedding. Chris is in front of the congregation, Adam is waiting with him, and Eve is walking up the aisle. However, she stops halfway, and tells Adam that she can't marry him because she's an heiress and she's afraid that he will get all of her money. Adam is about at his wit's end when Bernard stops forward and offers to help.

Bernard and Chris meet with Adam and Eve in a back room and Bernard prepares a standard preputial agreement. When they find out that Eve's net worth is twenty-two million dollars, they realize that the negotiations will take a while. While all this is going on, Maggie approaches Joel who is sitting alone outside. At Maggie's approach, Joel tells her not to start and says that he gives up and she wins. Maggie is confused by his response.

Joel tells her that whatever game they've been playing, Maggie is clearly the victor, and thinks that they should just draw a line in the sand and agree to stay on opposite sides of it. Maggie appears disappointed at this, and Joel reaffirms his seriousness. She finally tells Joel regretfully that she thinks he is a great kisser and smiles at him. Just then, Ed comes out and announces that the wedding will recommence.

The wedding ceremony completes without a problem. As Adam and Eve leave the church, Eve throws the bouquet over her shoulder. It falls in the middle of a crowd of people and as they step away, the bouquet is still lying on the ground. Everyone looks at it in horror, and quickly walks away.

"Cicely"

Guest Starring: Jo Anderson: Roslyn, Yvonne Suhor: Cicely, Roberts Blossom: Ned

Co-Starring: Peg Phillips: Rhoda, William J. White: Dave the Cook, Brian T. Finney: Singing Drunk, Sharon Collar: Thin Woman, Krisha Fairchild: Sturdy Woman

Written by: Diane Frolov and Andrew Schneider

Directed by: Rob Thompson

Joel is driving home late one night and almost hits an elderly man. The man falls and Joel helps him up and takes him to his cabin to look at the man's injured ankle. The man introduces himself as Ned Svenborg and explains that he moved away from Cicely back in 1909 and has not been back since. While Ned obviously has a great love for Cicely, Joel feels as if it were a hole in his life, sucking away for of his most precious years. Ned is disapproving of Joel's attitude and tells him a story about the foundation of Cicely.

As Ned tells the story, Joel imagines the various characters as incarnations of present-day inhabitants of Cicely. Ned describes himself as a boy living in squalor with no education or manners. The young Ned is seen as Ed, rolling in the dirt and begging for change. Mace Mobrey, the 1909 counterpart to Maurice, held the town in his grasp and was assisted by his hired gun Kit who appeared as Chris. Mace had possession of Sally, who was a young harlot resembling Shelly. However, Sally was secretly loved by Abe, who resembled Holling. The entire town was resigned to its lawlessness, save for Mary O'Keefe, a missionary woman with Maggie's face, who attempted rather unsuccessfully to convert the townspeople.

Joel remains doubtful of Ned's story but Ned tells Joel that two people together can work miracles. He tells of the first time he

ANSWERS ON PAGE 149

TRIVIA TEASERS: MISC

1) What is on the sign during the original ending credits?

2) What was Soapy Sanderson wearing when he dies?

3) What was Soapy's wife's name?

4) How long was Soapy married?

5) How old was Soapy when he died?

6) How long was Soapy a professor?

7) What doctorates did Soapy hold?

8) What wine did Soapy leave for Joel and Maggie?

9) How long has Adam been in Alaska?

10) What was Elizabeth Schroeder's maiden name?

11) How much did Elizabeth Schroeder's baby boy weigh?

12) Who has the beard, Erick or Ron?

13) What is the name of the inn run by Erick and Ron?

14) By which lake is the Inn located?

15) Who sent the package that went around the world?

16) When did he send it?

17) How old was he when he sent it?

18) What did Cicely put in the package?

19) Where did they send the package?

20) In which branch of the military did Erick serve?

21) What position did he hold in Japan?

22) When did Jack die?

23) What was stolen in the '88 meltdown?

24) What was stolen in '90?

25) What was stolen in '91?

26) What year was Ned born?

saw Cicely and Roslyn, who had just arrived in town. Roslyn was a tough muscular woman with an uncharacteristic kindness in her eyes. Her travelling partner was Cicely, a frail, fair-skinned figure of astonishing beauty. Roslyn was the first one to help Ed, lifting him up out of the mud and telling him to walk like a man. The two women entered the local tavern and Roslyn immediately established her authority, punching out a man who tried to stop the missionary woman from singing.

Ned tells Joel that Cicely and Roslyn were looking for an escape from society, and had a vision of a utopian society, where everyone was free to be their best. To that end, Roslyn began work on a salon, which would later become the Brick. The salon was build to allow a place for cultural expression to take place. Since Mace and Kit were out town, Abe took this opportunity to express his love for Sally who learned to love herself through him.

The salon opened on May first and the first performance was a dance by Cicely. Although the crowd was noisy and rude at first, Cicely's profound presence soon quieted them and Ned began to fall in love. Cicely took it upon herself to teach Ned how to read, and Ned finally expressed his love for Cicely. Cicely was flattered but her heart belonged to Roslyn. It was apparent that their serious relationship went beyond mere friendship.

Seasons passed and six months of cold winter went by. Roslyn was strong and survived well but she was concerned about Cicely, whose health was much more fragile. As spring arrived, so did new hope for the residents of Cicely. Franz Kafka, who had the appearance of Joel, arrived in town to meet with Roslyn and to hopefully cure his writer's block. With the help of Mary, he was able to establish the premise for his *Metamorphosis*, and the two of them began a lasting relationship.

At another performance, Ned read a poem he had written entitled, "Between Antigone." Although it was not a remarkable poem, the pride in Cicely's eyes was unmistakable, for Ned was her creation and he had made her proud. However, even in that moment of joy, Cicely began a deep and fitful coughing, the precursor to a tragic illness.

Laying in bed, Cicely's visage was pale and her eyes were sunken in dark circles. Roslyn offered to take her to the City of Angels is California, where the air is clear and it is always warm, but Cicely refused, saying, "This is our home." As Cicely's illness worsened, Roslyn began blaming herself for risking Cicely's life for the sake of her own dreams of art and self-expression. Yet Mary tried to explain that without art, life is not worth living. At the same moment, Kit arrived in town and was disturbed by the change which had occurred. When Sally refused to go with him to meet Mace, he became angry and promised that Mace would return and kill everybody who stood against him.

A town meeting was held by Ned to discuss their options. Many wanted to stand and fight but Roslyn said that they should all run away. At that moment Cicely walked in, pale and weak, but driven by an inner fire. She exclaimed that it was not a stupid dream, that they had created a society where all people are equal, and all are valued. She encouraged the freedom to express our art, and our love, and Roslyn looked at her with a deep respect and love. Then, as strong as she was one moment, she was suddenly weak, and was caught be several townspeople as she collapsed in a dead faint.

As Mace and his men rode into town, Roslyn had them surrounded. Roslyn wished to talk things out with Mace but he wouldn't listen. Just before the townspeople were about to fire on Mace, a lone gunner, who had gone unnoticed, fired a shot at Roslyn. Cicely saw the gunner a moment before and dove between him and Roslyn, taking the bullet in her own back. As her figure lay on the ground, Roslyn pleaded with Cicely not to leave her. But fate intervened, and as Cicely looked up into Roslyn's eyes, she died. The entire town forgot their disputes and at that moment, the town became Cicely.

After the funeral, Kafka and Mary moved off to Prague, and the rest of the town went on as normal. Roslyn however, withdrew into herself and one day left the town altogether, never to be seen again.

After Ned finishes his story, he tells Joel that this day would have been Cicely's one hundredth birthday and he has come to pay his respects. Joel drives him to the cemetery where Ned asks to be left alone. In town, Joel enters the Brick after closing time. As he sits thinking, he can hear the sounds of Cicely as it was back in 1909 and a faint smile crosses his lips.

TRIVIA QUIZ ANSWERS

JOEL

1) Flushing, New York

2) 139th and Main, by the Long Island railroad

3) Columbia University School of Physicians and Surgeons

4) Beth Zion hospital in New York City

5) Herb and Nadine

6) Katie Kaplan

7) Camp Indianhead

8) Richmond Hill High

9) Velachiske, Russia

10) Joel's grandfather, Jack

11) Naomi Fleischman of Brooklyn Heights

12) Yakovenyahoshika

13) His great-uncle Joel

14) "Heals With Tools"

15) Elaine Schulman

16) Brooklyn, New York

17) New York University

18) Charles and Maxine Schulman

19) Louie

20) Clem Tillman

21) A pastrami on rye from Stage Deli

22) "Who Put The Bomp"

23) "Stand By Me"

24) Dwight, a federal judge in Louisville

25) 12 years

26) "The Juggler"

27) 17

28) No

29) A turtle named Jimmy

JOEL/CICELY

1) 75

2) 74

3) The State of Alaska

4) $125,000

5) Four years

6) Peter Gilliam

7) Three years

TOWN OF CICELY

1) Cicely and Roslyn

2) Montana

3) 1892

4) The Borough of Arrowhead County

5) The state thought that Joel's name was "Joe", and the "L" had to be added on later.

6) A hippie passing through town

7) Maurice

8) The hippie was so doped up, he forgot to paint it, so Maurice had to paint it himself

9) Maggie O'Connell, Charles "Red" Murphy and Charlie Bates

10) Around 830

11) The Bearded Nail

12) May 1st, 1909

13) "North to the future"

14) 570 AM

15) 1932

MAGGIE

1) Mary Margaret

2) Grosse Pointe, Michigan

3) Frank O'Connell

4) The youngest CEO in automotive history

5) Jane O'Connell

6) 58

7) Pilot

8) Cessna 4423V

9) Prostitute

10) Little Miss Great Lakes

11) A trick knee

12) Darvon

13) Dave, a graduate student

14) Mountain of My Misgivings

15) Mountain climbing

16) He fell asleep on a glacier and froze to death

17) He fell off of a mountain

18) In his Volvo, he took a wrong turn

onto a missile test site

19) Food poisoning from potato salad

20) Rick Pederson

21) No

22) R.E.M.—Green

23) He was hit by a falling satellite

24) Cordelaine

MAURICE

1) 53

2) Astronaut

3) Yes

4) Bought 15,000 acres of land

5) Started a radio station and a newspaper

6) Malcolm P. Minnifield

7) Outside Knoxville, Tennessee

8) The "Alaskan Riviera"

9) "Hello Young Lovers"

10) "The King And I"

11) Gus Grissom: Guys and Dolls
    John Glenn: Brigadoon
    Scotty Carpenter: West Side Story

12) Old Spice

13) A 2-inch birthmark in the shape of Madagascar on his upper right trapezius

14) McAllister

15) 16

16) He forged his father's signature

17) Highlander

18) North Dakota

19) June '89

20) Emperor Hirohito

21) It was a gift from a dealership in Houston, for riding the top of a rocket

HOLLING

1) The Yukon

2) January 1, 1929

3) Gustav

4) 104

5) 42

6) 106

7) 44

8) Celeste

9) Charlie

10) 110

11) De Vincoeur

12) Claude

13) Ten feet tall, 1800 pounds

14) Holling bit it off

15) 1988

16) Summer of 1984

17) 133

18) Fritz Heiman

SHELLY

1) Saskatoon, Saskatchewan, Canada

2) Wayne Jones
3) 20

4) Miss Northwest Passage

5) Maurice

6) Gorman Tambo

7) Tammy Tambo

8) Four times

9) "I Did It My Way"

10) Marge

11) Kyle Butler

12) Angel

13) Cindy

14) Saskatchewan College of Fine Arts

15) Hair, and Base Application

CHRIS
1) Wheeling, West Virginia

2) July 3, 1963

3) Auto body work

4) Pastor

5) He answered a classified in the back of Rolling Stone

6) Bernard Stevens

7) July 3, 1963

8) Portland, Oregon

9) 42

10) Roy Bauer

11) 43

12) Kicknuck Lake

13) Leslie Ferguson

ED
1) Wrapped in a sealskin coat

2) She was a white woman, and a missionary

3) Smith

4) Fairbanks

MARILYN
1) Leonard Quinhagak

2) Healer

3) Since he was twelve

RUTH-ANNE
1) Miller

2) 75

3) 1971, in a '61 DeSoto

4) Bill

5) Rudy and Matthew

6) He lives in Portland and drives a truck

7) He lives in Chicago and is an investment banker

MISC
1) "Off Season Snow Moblie Sale"

2) Old Spice

3) Helen

4) 42 years

5) 82 years old

6) 20 years

7) Theology and Mythology

8) Lafitte Rothschild 1975

9) 15 years

10) Carrey

11) Six pounds, nine ounces

12) Ron

13) The Sourdough Inn

14) Eagle Lake

15) Richard McWilliams

16) June 8th, 1988

17) Eight years old

18) A thermometer

19) Barwana, India

20) The Marine Corps

21) Guard at the Tokyo Embassy

22) 1948

23) Electric toothbrushes

24) Hair dryers

25) Radios

26) 1884

hotos by Anita J. Micuel

Pioneer Books wants to be your entertainment book company and make you happy by producing the best books we can about your favorite subjects. Your voice is important in choosing which books we publish. Please complete this questionairre and either photocopy it or tear it out and send it back to us. Your help is greatly appreciated!

Is your first Pioneer book? yes____   no____   What Pioneer book(s) do you have?_____

How did you hear about our books?_____

Rate the book(s) on a scale of 1-5 (5 being the highest)____

How could we make the book(s) better?_____

Other than bookstores and mail order, where else would you like to be able to purchase our books (i.e. gift

shops, Walmart, Target, K-MART)?_____

Why did you purchase the book(s) (ie gift, personal, job related)?_____

What publications do you subscribe to or read on a regular basis?_____

What are your favorite T.V. shows?_____

What other books would you like to see us publish?_____

Couch Potato carries a full line of Pioneer Books. Would you like to be added to the list to receive notice of upcoming new releases and a free catalog of all titles? yes____   no____

Name _____   Age: 18-25____ 26-35____ 36-45____ 45+____

Address: _____

Occupation _____   Education: High School____ College_____ Adv. Degree_____

Yearly Earnings: under $25,000____ $25,000-$50,000____ $50,000+__   Sex: male____ female____

Please add any other comments you may have:

THANK YOU VERY MUCH!

David Marin

Northern Exposure

TREK: THE UNAUTHORIZED BEHIND-THE-SCENES STORY OF THE NEXT GENERATION

James VanHise

This book chronicles the Trek mythos as it continues on T.V. in "Star Trek: The Next Generation," telling the often fascinating conflict filled story of the behind-the-scenes struggles between Roddenberry and the creative staff. It includes a special section on "Star Trek: Deep Space Nine," a spin-off of "The Next Generation," which will begin syndication in early 1993.

$14.95.....160 Pages
ISBN 1-55698-321-2

THE NEW TREK ENCYCLOPEDIA

John Peel with Scott Nance

Everything anyone might want to know about the Star Trek series of television shows and movies is conveniently compiled into one volume in *The New Trek Encyclopedia*.

This detailed volume covers the original T.V. series, all six feature films, "Star Trek: The Next Generation," and the animated show. It provides descriptions, explanations, and important details of every alien race, monster, planet, spaceship, weapon, and technical device to appear in all the shows—all listed in alphabetical order for easy reference. It also includes every person who worked on the shows or movies!

$19.95.....300 Pages
ISBN 1-55698-350-6

COUCH POTATO INC.   5715 N. Balsam Rd   Las Vegas, NV 89130   (702)658-2090

Use Your Credit Card 24 HRS — Order toll Free From: **(800)444-2524** Ext 67

MAKING A QUANTUM LEAP

Scott Nance

Everything you ever wanted to know about "Quantum Leap" is in this exciting new book! Learn how the series was created, how each story is filmed, and meet stars Scott Bakula, Dean Stockwell, and the writers and directors behind the hit.

$14.95.....160 Pages
ISBN # 1-55698-312-3

THE UNOFFICIAL TALE OF BEAUTY AND THE BEAST

Revised 2nd Edition   Edward Gross

THE UNOFFICIAL TALE OF BEAUTY AND THE BEAST is the ultimate "bible" to the series, providing in-depth interviews with story editor-producer Howard Gordon, Directors Paul Lynch, Alan Cooke and Richard Franklin; a look at the creation of the series and an incredibly detailed episode guide. This revised second edition adds an interview with Ron Perlman, who has captured the hearts of millions via his portrayal of the noble lion-man, Vincent and an interview with actor Tony Jay, best known as Underworld villian, Paracelsus.

$14.95.....164 Pages
ISBN # 1-55698-261-5

THE ADDAMS FAMILY REVEALED
James Van Hise

* One of the most popular series in television history recently released as a Major motion picture

Beginning with a detailed biography of Charles Addams, the creator of the panel cartoon that led to the television show, this book traces the entire story of Gomez, Morticia, and the rest of the happy crew from the earliest television episodes to the new feature film.

$14.95.....164 Pages
ISBN # 1-55698-300-X

BLOODSUCKER: Vampires at the Movies
Scott Nance

All the great neck-biters are here!

Bloodsuckers traces the onscreen legacy of cinematic vampires from the first major film treatment, F.W. Murnau's 1922 silent classic, *Nosferatu*. The book examines the evolution of the vampire through the "Dark Shadows" series, the Frank Langella *Dracula*, the upcoming adaptation of the bestseller *The Vampire Lestat,* and more!

$14.95.....160 Pages
ISBN # 1-55698-317-4

COUCH POTATO INC.   5715 N. Balsam Rd   Las Vegas, NV 89130   (702)658-2090

Use Your Credit Card 24 HRS — Order toll Free From: **(800)444-2524** Ext 67

BATMANIA II
James Van Hise

Tracing the Batman phenomenon over the past fifty years, beginning with the characters creation by Bob Kane in 1939, and examining the changes in the pages of Detective Comics and his own title over the last five decades. Then the focus shifts to the two movie serials and jumps two decades to the enormously popular BATMAN television series of the 1960's, the primary focus of the book. Includes coverage of both new movies with Michael Keaton.

Interviews with Adam West (Batman), Burt Ward (Robin), Yvonne Craig (Batgirl), Julie Newmar (The Catwoman), writer Stanley Ralph Ross and George Barris, who designed the various Bat-vehicles, bring the reader behind the scenes. Special sections showcase the innumerable collectibles inspired by the show, and the ongoing phenomenon that surrounds it.

$14.95.....164 Pages
ISBN # 1-55698-315-8

THE GREEN HORNET
James Van Hise

Batman was not the only superhero television series to air in the 1960's. Its creators also brought ABC's THE GREEN HORNET, which starred Van Williams as the Green Hornet with martial arts superstar Bruce Lee as his sidekick, Kato, to the screen.

A guide to every episode of the television series, with actor and character profiles make this a complete look at this unique super hero.

$14.95.......120 Pages

SPECIAL OFFER: A limited edition volume combining the books on THE GREEN HORNET television series and the movie serial. This two-in-one book is only $16.95

BORING, BUT NECESSARY ORDERING INFORMATION

Payment:
Use our new 800 # and pay with your credit card or send check or money order directly to our address. All payments must be made in U.S. funds and please do not send cash.

Shipping:
We offer several methods of shipment. Sometimes a book can be delayed if we are temporarily out of stock. You should note whether you prefer us to ship the book as soon as available, send you a merchandise credit good for other goodies, or send your money back immediately.

Normal Post Office: $3.75 for the first book and $1.50 for each additional book. These orders are filled as quickly as possible. Shipments normally take 5 to 10 days, but allow up to 12 weeks for delivery.

Special UPS 2 Day Blue Label Service or Priority Mail: Special service is available for desperate Couch Potatoes. These books are shipped within 24 hours of when we receive the order and normally take 2 to 3 three days to get to you. The cost is $10.00 for the first book and $4.00 each additional book .

Overnight Rush Service: $20.00 for the first book and $10.00 each additional book.

U.s. Priority Mail: $6.00 for the first book and $3.00.each additional book.

Canada And Mexico: $5.00 for the first book and $3.00 each additional book.

Foreign: $6.00 for the first book and $3.00 each additional book.

Please list alternatives when available and please state if you would like a refund or for us to backorder an item if it is not in stock.

COUCH POTATO INC.   5715 N. Balsam Rd   Las Vegas, NV 89130   (702)658-2090

Use Your Credit Card 24 HRS — Order toll Free From: **(800)444-2524** Ext 67

ORDER FORM

_____ Trek Crew Book $9.95
_____ Best Of Enterprise Incidents $9.95
_____ Trek Fans Handbook $9.95
_____ Trek: The Next Generation $14.95
_____ The Man Who Created Star Trek: $12.95
_____ 25th Anniversary Trek Tribute $14.95
_____ History Of Trek $14.95
_____ The Man Between The Ears $14.95
_____ Trek: The Making Of The Movies $14.95
_____ Trek: The Lost Years $12.95
_____ Trek: The Unauthorized Next Generation $14.95
_____ New Trek Encyclopedia $19.95
_____ Making A Quantum Leap $14.95
_____ The Unofficial Tale Of Beauty And The Beast $14.95
_____ Complete Lost In Space $19.95
_____ ..doctor Who Encyclopedia: Baker $19.95
_____ Lost In Space Tribute Book $14.95
_____ Lost In Space With Irwin Allen $14.95
_____ Doctor Who: Baker Years $19.95
_____ Doctor Who: Pertwee Years $19.95
_____ Batmania Ii $14.95
_____ The Green Hornet $14.95 _____ Special Edition $16.95

_____ Number Six: The Prisoner Book $14.95
_____ Gerry Anderson: Supermarionation $17.95
_____ Addams Family Revealed $14.95
_____ Bloodsucker: Vampires At The Movies $14.95
_____ Dark Shadows Tribute $14.95
_____ Monsterland Fear Book $14.95
_____ The Films Of Elvis $14.95
_____ The Woody Allen Encyclopedia $14.95
_____ Paul Mccartney: 20 Years On His Own $9.95
_____ Yesterday: My Life With The Beatles $14.95
_____ Fab Films Of The Beatles $14.95
_____ 40 Years At Night: The Tonight Show $14.95
_____ Exposing Northern Exposure $14.95
_____ The La Lawbook $14.95
_____ Cheers: Where Everybody Knows Your Name $14.95
_____ SNL! The World Of Saturday Night Live $14.95
_____ The Rockford Phile $14.95
_____ Encyclopedia Of Cartoon Superstars $14.95
_____ How To Create Animation $14.95
_____ How To Draw Art For Comic Books $14.95
_____ King And Barker:an Illustrated Guide $14.95
_____ King And Barker: An Illustrated Guide II $14.95

100% Satisfaction Guaranteed.

We value your support. You will receive a full refund as long as the copy of the book you are not happy with is received back by us in reasonable condition. No questions asked, except we would like to know how we failed you. Refunds and credits are given as soon as we receive back the item you do not want.

NAME:_____

STREET:_____

CITY:_____

STATE:_____

ZIP:_____

TOTAL:_____ SHIPPING_____

NEXP

SEND TO: Couch Potato, Inc. 5715 N. Balsam Rd., Las Vegas, NV 89130